super **soups**

super soups

michael van straten

TED SMART

Dedication

In the most loving memory of my mother, Kitty: I'll always remember
that wonderful aroma as I arrived home from school to see her
making chicken soup.

Super Soups

by Michael van Straten

First published in Great Britain in 2002 by
Mitchell Beazley, an imprint of Octopus Publishing
Group Limited, 2–4 Heron Quays, London E14 4JP.

A CIP catalogue record for this book is available from the British Library.

ISBN: 1 84000 700 1

The author and publishers will be grateful for any information that will assist them in keeping
future editions up-to-date. Although all reasonable care has been taken in the preparation of this
book, neither the publishers, editors nor the author can accept any liability for any consequences arising from the use thereof, or the
information contained therein.

This edition produced for The Book People Ltd, Hall Wood Avenue, Haydock, St Helens WA11 9UL

Commissioning Editor: Hilary Lumsden
Executive Art Editor: Yasia Williams
Senior Editor: Lara Maiklem
Editor: Jamie Ambrose
Design: Grade Design Consultants
Photographer: Nicki Dowey
Production: Kieran Connelly
Index: Hilary Bird

Typeset in Myriad MM

Printed and bound by Toppan Printing Company in China

Contents

Introduction

"It's good soup, and not fine words, that keeps me alive." *Molière, 1672*

Just thinking of the word "soup" conjures up mental images of a family kitchen from bygone days: a huge pot bubbling on the stove, wonderful aromas wafting through the house, and the instant welling-up of happiness and appetite. All over the world, soup is basic food, and has been since the earliest recipes were documented. Long before there were written records, soups appeared in drawings and paintings. From the hearty, thick-enough-to-stand-a-spoon-in soups of northern and eastern Europe to the subtle, delicate flavours of Asia, soup has long been a staple food for almost every culture.

Fish soups from all over the Mediterranean, chowders from America, bean and pasta soups from Italy, traditional French onion soup, recipes adapted from former colonies (such as the Indian influence in mulligatawny)… these are not only wonderful dishes to eat, but they're healing dishes as well. Whether you want a substantial meal-in-a-bowl on a cold winter's evening or the most delicate, crystal-clear broth as an appetizing starter to your light summer supper, the super soups in this book will fulfil the needs of both your taste buds and your health.

Some of the earliest written recipes come from the pen of the great Roman gourmet Apicius, thanks to whom we have the details of the culinary traditions of ancient Rome and Greece. More than 2,000 years later, it is fascinating to discover that the cooks of the classical world were using cloves, ginger, cardamom, nutmeg, pepper, and cinnamon – and that they understood the medicinal value of these exotic spices. Maybe their Roman chicken broth was the forerunner of the now-famous "Jewish penicillin" (chicken soup), or perhaps the original version of my bean and barley soup could have been eaten by

Julius Caesar, when it might have contained chickpeas, lentils, barley, leeks, coriander, aniseed, fennel, oregano, lovage, and cabbage. Today, a bowl of super soup is still a welcome treat, whether hot and warming in winter or chilled and refreshing on a hot summer's day. But if the only soup you have ever tasted comes out of a carton, a can or – heaven forbid – a packet of powder, you don't know what you're missing. If these are your staples as far as soup is concerned, you're certainly getting far too much salt (which will push up your blood pressure), probably spoonfuls of chemical additives, and definitely far less health-promoting nourishment than you would from any of the recipes included in this book.

Besides the obvious flavour and health benefits, nothing you do in the kitchen engenders the feeling of caring and loving as much as making soup. Paul McCartney once said that he'd rather have a bowl of his late wife Linda's soup than eat at the poshest restaurant in London. I agree with him about the soup – my wife Sally's soups certainly keep me at home. Many people are put off soup-making because they think it's too complicated. Let me assure you: nothing is simpler than super soup-making. It's quick, easy, and can be incredibly inexpensive besides. In terms of nutritional value for money, homemade soup must be the best of all health bargains. Not only do you get a bowlful of protective vitamins and minerals, body-building protein, and energy-giving complex carbohydrates, but you also benefit from enzymes and plant chemicals that improve digestion, boost resistance, and fight off infections.

So don't waste a minute: go to the shops now, then get into the kitchen and start cooking. All the recipes serve four people. Once you've tasted the results of these deliciously simple super-soup recipes, you'll soon become a dedicated soup-maker – and a promoter of good health into the bargain.

Sou

p Basics

The soup-maker's kitchen

For some reason I've never understood, soup-making seems to have acquired the mystical qualities of Macbeth's three witches. Believe me: you don't need a coven or strange parts of unspeakable animals to make great soups. What you do need are good-quality ingredients, a chopping board, sharp knives, and a decent, thick-bottomed saucepan. Amazing machines can make the process easier, but you can still make wonderful soup without them.

The store cupboard

My friend the great chef Raymond Blanc told me that with two carrots, an onion, and a few fresh herbs, he could make a soup fit for a king. And it's true: the beauty of soup-making is that you can use practically anything to create delicious results. The Brussels sprouts and Stilton left over the day after Christmas, what's left of your roast chicken, the outer leaves of a cabbage, that parsnip you didn't get round to using, a half-empty bag of frozen peas, even the red peppers left over from a salad… you can use them all.

In order to make the best use of such leftovers, however, you do need to keep some staple items on hand. Essentials include a few cans of beans, tomatoes, and chickpeas, tomato purée, some packets of lentils, red and yellow split peas, a tub of low-salt, organic vegetable and herb granules, and finally, yeast and herb extract – the Swiss-made Bioforce and Marigold brands are the best. Herbs are essential, too, and fresh are definitely best. If you grow your own, most can be frozen in ice-cube trays and added as required, but do keep a supply of dried bouquets garnis, sage, thyme, bay, oregano, *fines herbes*, chillies, and your other favourites on hand. Keep some fresh garlic and onions in your store cupboard as well.

Gadgets

If you're serious about soup, it's worth buying a decent stockpot with a basket; otherwise, you'll need a big, fine-meshed strainer. Blenders make soup-making easier and quicker, and they needn't cost the earth. A hand-held wand blender costs around £10 ($14.50). If you have more money available, choose from a wide variety of standard blenders. The best is undoubtedly the American-made KitchenAid (although it is also the most expensive). Another really good gadget is the hand-held Bamix. Swiss engineering makes this a chopper, blender, mixer, and mincer which will also purée soup. At around £80 ($116), it's not cheap – but it is very popular with professional chefs.

The best gadget of all is the German Thermomix. This is a combined food processor, cooker, and steamer with which you can make fabulous soup, all in one container, from start to finish. It will also make jam in twenty minutes, sorbets in two, and bread dough, batter, and sauces at the push of a couple of buttons. It does cost more than £500 ($725), but if you're a serious cook, it will last a lifetime and give you endless pleasure.

When it comes to knives, chopping boards, and other cooking paraphernalia, the best value for money (and widest selection) I've found comes from Lakeland Limited, which has twenty-five shops around Britain, and a good internet site (www.lakelandlimited.com). I've tried most brands of knives on the market, but those that are head and shoulders above the rest are made in Japan by NipponKitchen. They hold their edges much longer than other knives. If you want the best, then these are certainly worth the money.

Stock basics

Most people believe that they don't have enough time to make simple soups, let alone the time to make stock. While it is true that making your own stocks can be time-consuming, believe me, it is worth the effort. Of course, you can use the ever-popular stock cubes, but generally they contain far too much salt and a wide range of chemical preservatives, flavourings, colourings, and hydrogenated fats you and your family would be better off without. Happily, organic varieties are now available – there are even some low-salt, organic products, too. So if you must use a stock cube for convenience, choose the healthier options from health-food stores or supermarket shelves.

In the convenience world of the twenty-first century, it is also possible to buy "fresh" stock alongside the "fresh" cartons of soup in most supermarkets. These are certainly an improvement on stock cubes and powdered or canned soups, but they are extremely expensive, still far too salty, and not a patch on the genuine article that you can easily make in the most basic of kitchens. After all, it's not so long since our ancestors did it all in an iron pot on a cooking range fuelled with wood or coal. You can use stock cubes or cartoned stock for all the recipes in this book, but if you want your super soups to have the maximum health-giving impact, good homemade stock is fundamental.

The reason? Even the healthiest and best of the available instant products lack the nutritional quality and flavour that come from using homemade stock, so if you do nothing else with this book, at least try the vegetable stock recipe on page 13; it couldn't be simpler. Take a few hours to brew up a giant potful, then concentrate it by boiling it down to half its volume. Once it has cooled, freeze it in ice-cube trays, then empty the cubes into a double freezer bag, making sure to label and date it. You can keep liquid stock in the fridge for a couple of weeks, or in the freezer for a couple of months.

When you need the stock for soups, sauces or gravies, use each cube with the same amount of water. A rough guide is half-a-dozen cubes in a casserole or stew, a couple with the vegetable water to make gravy, three or four with boiling water for risotto, or as many as you need to make up the stock for the following recipes. You can do exactly the same with chicken, beef, fish, and ham stocks to bring back the traditional flavour and health-giving benefits of the stockpot to your kitchen.

The stock recipes on the following pages are my own personal favourites.

The healthiest base for most super soup recipes

Vegetable stock

When I was a child, mothers, grandmothers, and elderly maiden aunts insisted that children drink the vegetable cooking water (I know mine all did): not a drop was ever wasted, as all of it went into soups, sauces, gravies, and casseroles. As with many old wives' tales, there was sound reasoning behind this practice: the cooking water is nutrient-rich, containing vitamins, minerals, and enzymes leached out of the vegetables during the boiling process.

Making your own vegetable stock is the equivalent of concocting five-star, health-promoting vegetable water. All the protective nutrients in onions and leeks; betacarotenes for natural resistance, healthy skin, and eyesight in carrots; and heart-protective potassium in the parsnips: all are abundant in vegetable stock. In this recipe, there's also added value from the essential oils in the sage, thyme, and bay leaves.

2 onions, 1 peeled and quartered, 1 left whole with the skin on

3 large stalks of celery

2 large carrots, trimmed and peeled if not organic, sliced roughly

1 large leek, washed and sliced

1 large parsnip, trimmed and peeled if not organic

1 large sprig of sage

2 sprigs of thyme

6 bay leaves

1 small bunch of parsley

About 1 litre OR 35fl oz water

8 black peppercorns

Half a teaspoon salt

Put all the ingredients into a large saucepan – or ideally, a pasta pan with a fitted sieve.

Bring slowly to the boil.

Simmer for about an hour.

Remove the pasta sieve or strain through kitchen muslin or a sieve, pressing the vegetable pulp with a wooden spoon.

For all-over protection and good digestion; essential in fish cookery

Fish stock

Homemade fish stock tastes absolutely stunning and will impart a uniquely professional flavour to all fish and shellfish soups, sauces, and risottos. It is rich in iodine, a mineral often deficient in modern diets and essential for the normal function of the thyroid gland. The protective benefits of onions and leeks, combined with the digestion-improving essential oils from mint and tarragon, make this a healthy base for all your fish cookery.

100g OR 3½oz fish trimmings and bones (most supermarkets offering a filleting service will keep bones, heads, and trimmings if given a day's notice)

3 carrots, trimmed and peeled if not organic, cubed

2 sweet, white, Spanish onions, peeled and coarsely chopped

1 large leek, washed and coarsely chopped

1 large sprig of rosemary

1 medium bunch of parsley

1 medium bunch of mint

3 large sprigs of tarragon

1.5 litres OR 55fl oz water, or 1 litre OR 35fl oz water and 500ml OR 18fl oz dry white wine

8 white peppercorns

Half a teaspoon salt

Put the washed and dried fish trimmings in a large saucepan.

Add the rest of the ingredients and bring to the boil slowly.

Simmer for about thirty minutes, skimming the surface regularly.

Strain through kitchen muslin or a fine sieve.

An all-round healthy stock with plenty of vitamin content

Chicken stock

After vegetable stock, this is probably the most useful stock recipe. Because it's fairly neutral in flavour, good chicken stock can be substituted for beef or ham stock. It is particularly good for making most soups and risottos, and is perfectly acceptable as the base for most sauces and gravies – unless, of course, you're cooking for vegetarians.

A good chicken stock is a valuable source of enzymes and B vitamins, as well as the mood-enhancing essential oils found in rosemary and sage, and the protective plant chemicals found in onions, leeks, thyme, and bay leaves.

1 chicken carcass (your butcher may sell them after cutting off the legs, drumsticks, and breasts for other customers; otherwise, do it yourself or use the leftovers from roast chicken)

2 litres OR 70fl oz water

6 spring onions, green tips left on

1 large leek, trimmed, washed, and coarsely chopped

2 large stalks of celery, chopped

1 large sprig of rosemary

Half a large bunch of parsley

1 large sprig of sage

2 large sprigs of thyme

3 bay leaves

10 white peppercorns

About ⅓ teaspoon salt

Put the chicken carcass in a large saucepan. Cover with the water.

Bring to the boil and simmer for about thirty minutes.

Add the rest of the ingredients.

Bring back to the boil and simmer for forty minutes.

Strain through kitchen muslin or a sieve.

The digestible choice for pork-based soups

Ham stock

The robust flavour of ham stock is perfect for recipes such as Dutch pea soup with smoked sausage, cabbage soup with gammon, or chickpea and spicy sausage – in fact, any soup which uses pork. It's also perfect for making white sauce to go with boiled gammon or ham – and, naturally, forms the ideal base for the gravy to pour over roast pork. The addition of cloves and allspice in this recipe helps the digestion of the slightly higher fat content of pork and its related products.

About 900g OR 2lb ham bones

2 large red onions, peeled and coarsely chopped

2 large carrots, trimmed and peeled if not organic, coarsely chopped

1 large leek, washed and coarsely chopped

2 large sticks of celery, chopped

6 cloves

1 teaspoon allspice

5 bay leaves

10 black peppercorns

2 litres OR 70fl oz water

Half a teaspoon salt

Put all of the ingredients into a large saucepan.

Bring to the boil and simmer slowly for about four hours, skimming regularly with a slotted spoon to remove the fat.

Strain through kitchen muslin or a sieve.

Leave, covered, until completely cold.

Skim off any solidified fat.

The proper stuff: with great flavour and no danger of chemicals or BSE

Beef stock

The true flavour of beef stock is the most difficult of all to reproduce as a stock cube without the addition of chemical additives, especially the awful monosodium glutamate. The delicate and unique taste of homemade beef stock is one of the most glorious delights of the kitchen, as well as being the cheapest – your butcher will normally give you the bones for nothing when you buy other meat or poultry.

It is vital, however, to obtain bones from organically reared beef, as they will have a better flavour and contain no chemical additives, growth hormones or BSE.

About 900g OR 2lb meat bones, sawn into 4 cm OR 1½-inch pieces by your butcher

2 large red onions, peeled and coarsely chopped

2 large carrots, trimmed and peeled if not organic, coarsely chopped

1 large leek, washed and coarsely chopped

2 large sticks of celery, chopped

1 large bunch of sage

1 stick of rosemary

5 bay leaves

10 black peppercorns

2 litres OR 70fl oz water

Half a teaspoon salt

Roast the meat bones for about thirty minutes at 220°C OR 450°F OR gas mark 7.

Put them and any scrapings into a large saucepan.

Add the rest of the ingredients.

Bring to the boil and simmer slowly for about four hours, skimming regularly with a slotted spoon to remove the fat.

Strain through kitchen muslin or a sieve.

Leave, covered, until completely cold.

Skim off any solidified fat.

Immu
bo

ne-osting Soups

For generations, the wonderful healers who have inhabited kitchens throughout the world have known about the health-boosting properties of soup. Made properly, soup contains some of the most powerful ingredients that can be used in what is often referred to as "kitchen medicine".

Unfortunately, however (and detrimentally to us all), within the rarified, scientific atmosphere of late twentieth-century western medical practice, the whole idea of food as medicine became viewed as backward, superstitious or even downright ridiculous.

Happily, twenty-first century medicine has a taken a much more enlightened approach to the subject. Today, a growing body of scientific evidence backs up the ancient idea that "we are what we eat". Many scientific studies have shown that common foods do indeed have the ability to kill off harmful bacteria and fungal infections. Phytochemicals – natural substances that occur in plants – exert a wide range of beneficial actions on the body, some of them concerned specifically with boosting natural immunity.

In our modern world, the body's immune system is under constant attack from pollutants, pesticides, herbicides, fungicides, and all the chemical detritus of so-called civilization. For this reason, it is even more important that highly protective antioxidant nutrients feature as widely as possible in day-to-day meals – which is precisely why the following Super Soups recipes were included in this book. All the soups in this chapter can directly improve and boost your body's natural defences to infection and damage, so it is vital to have them on a regular basis. When there's an epidemic of flu, colds or chest infections, use them more often to ensure that you escape whichever bug is doing the rounds.

Even if you have picked up an infection, immune-boosting soups are still essential eating, as they help shorten the duration of your illness.

The soups in this chapter rely heavily on the foods richest in the natural chemicals that help the body protect itself by safeguarding its cells. Cabbage, for example, is full of cancer-fighting phytochemicals as well as natural sulphur, which is antibacterial. Onions, garlic, and leeks contain powerful sulphurous allicins: substances that attack bacteria, viruses, and fungi. Poultry such as chicken and duck contain enzymes and B vitamins that enhance immunity. And all the bright-green, -yellow, and -orange vegetables are a major source of carotenoids, natural pigments that play an important role in good health.

When reading this chapter, don't be put off by seemingly strange combinations or unfamiliar foods in some of the recipes. You may think, for instance, that prunes are an odd ingredient to include in a soup (*see* Duck soup with prunes, page 31), but in fact they are one of nature's richest sources of antioxidants. Few people get enough of these powerful immune-boosting substances, yet we all need them in abundance as part of our constant fight against infection, disease, and illness.

Most of the herbs and spices in the recipes are included for their flavour, but they play health-giving roles as well. Bay leaves, thyme, rosemary, chillies, and oregano are all rich in volatile essential oils, substances that stimulate immune activity. This means that the blood's protective white cells are encouraged to attack and destroy invading organisms.

For all their scientific-sounding benefits, immune-boosting soups take us back to the roots of peasant cooking: they're easy to prepare, inexpensive to make, and simply bursting with flavour, nutrients, and everything you need for bodily self-defence. This is the true essence of kitchen medicine – thankfully, something most people today consider merits much more than ridicule.

Creamy watercress soup

In addition to having a wonderful peppery flavour, watercress is one of the most important immune-protectors you can eat. If you are a smoker, eat this soup twice a week, as it may well reduce your chances of lung cancer. There's an additional benefit from the protective probiotic bacteria in live yoghurt. It is well known that these "good bugs" are not only a part of the body's natural defences, but they also release specific chemicals that enhance the effectiveness of the immune system.

100g OR 3½ oz unsalted butter

4 large spring onions, trimmed, cleaned, and finely sliced

1 large bunch or bag of watercress – about 350g OR 12oz

1 litre OR 35fl oz vegetable stock (*see* page 13)

Bouquet garni: 3 sprigs each parsley, thyme, and rosemary, tied together with string, or a good commercial bouquet garni bag

200ml OR 7fl oz plain bio-yoghurt

In a large pan, melt the butter, then gently sweat the onions for three minutes.

Pull the leaves off any thick watercress stalks; discard the thicker stalks.

Add the watercress to the pan and stir briskly for one minute.

Add the stock and bouquet garni.

Simmer for ten minutes, then remove the bouquet garni.

Liquidize until smooth and return to the pan.

Add the yoghurt and stir thoroughly.

Serve hot with herb croutons (*see* page 128). Alternatively, serve cold as a delicious summer soup.

To protect the lungs …

Watercress contains

antibacterial mustard oils,

lots of betacarotene, and a phytochemical

that protects the cells of lung tissue against the

carcinogenic effects of smoking

White onion soup

Onions have a long tradition in folk medicine, particularly for helping the body overcome the effects of chest infections. In this recipe, this healing property is combined with the protective essential oils from bay leaves, thyme, and rosemary to make a delicious and health-giving, flavour-packed soup.

55g OR 2oz unsalted butter

500g OR 1 lb 2oz white Spanish onions, peeled and very finely sliced

3 level tablespoons flour

1 litre OR 35fl oz full-cream milk

4 bay leaves

10 peppercorns, slightly crushed

Bouquet garni: 3 sprigs each parsley, thyme, and rosemary, tied together with string, or a good commercial bouquet garni bag

1 medium bunch of flat-leaf parsley, washed and finely chopped

Melt the butter over a very low heat.

Add the onions. Cover and stir until thoroughly coated, then allow to sweat gently for ten minutes.

Sift in the flour and continue cooking for a further five minutes, stirring continuously.

Pour in the milk and add the bay leaves, peppercorns, and bouquet garni.

Simmer very gently for about ten minutes, until the onions are quite soft.

Remove the bay leaves and bouquet garni, and strain out the peppercorns.

Serve garnished generously with chopped parsley and rouille (*see* page 129) or potato floaters (*see* page 131).

For fighting chest infections …

Onions offer

antiviral and antibacterial protection

Parsley, offer

a diuretic, aids the natural cleansing process

Chinese pak choi and chicken

Pak choi is another member of the cabbage family that offers good all-round protection from germs. The good news is that this tasty vegetable is now widely available and is easy to prepare. When combined with the immune-boosting spring onions, garlic, and chicken stock in this recipe, it creates a power-packed super soup that provides a real boost to your system.

6 large spring onions

4 tablespoons rapeseed (canola) oil

2 cloves of garlic, peeled and crushed

1.2 litres OR 40fl oz chicken stock

2 chicken breasts, skinned and shredded finely along the grain of the flesh

4 heads of pak choi, thick stems removed and reserved, the leaves finely chopped

150g OR 5½ oz Chinese noodles or vermicelli (optional)

1 teaspoon tamari or light soy sauce

Chop the white parts of four of the spring onions very finely; cut the others lengthwise almost to the root and reserve.

Heat the oil very gently. Add the chopped onion and garlic and sweat for just two minutes.

Pour in the stock. Bring slowly to a simmer and remove the garlic.

Continuing to simmer, add the chicken and reserved pak choi stems, and cook for ten minutes, until the chicken is almost tender.

Remove the pak choi stems.

Add the pak choi leaves, noodles or vermicelli, and tamari or soy sauce and simmer for five minutes.

Serve with the reserved spring onions and rice fritters (*see* page 130) floating on top.

To strengthen the immune system …

Pak choi contains protective

thiocyanates, and large amounts of

betacarotene

for good cell health

Bread and garlic soup

There are many variations of this soup throughout Spain, and to judge from the number I've tried, every family must have its own favourite recipe. This is mine. If garlic's potency puts you off, take heart: cooking it this way seems to prevent the residual garlic breath, so be brave and give it a try if you want a bowlful of super immunity.

5 tablespoons olive oil

1 medium head of garlic, split into cloves, peeled, and finely chopped

4 thick slices of wholemeal bread (crusts removed), made into breadcrumbs

1.5 litres OR 55fl oz vegetable stock (*see* page 13)

Half a handful fresh oregano or 2 generous pinches of the dried herb

4 medium organic eggs

Heat the oil gently in a large pan.

Add the chopped garlic and sweat slowly, covered, for three minutes.

Tip in the breadcrumbs, vegetable stock, and oregano.

Keep covered and simmer for two minutes, adding more stock if the mixture gets too thick.

Beat the eggs. Add to the pan and simmer very gently for two more minutes.

Serve with herb croutons (*see* page 128).

To help fight bacteria …

Garlic contains powerful **antibacterial substances**

Oregano adds antiseptic **thymol**

Eggs provide health-giving **B vitamins**

Welsh minestrone with rice and leeks

The Roman emperor Nero used to eat leeks every day to protect his voice. It's no wonder that this vegetable is the national emblem of Wales, a nation renowned for its singing. When coughs, cold, flu, and sore throats abound, nothing could be better than this wonderfully thick cornucopia of germ-fighting nutrients. What's more, it tastes terrific.

3 tablespoons extra-virgin olive oil

3 Welsh onions (OR 1 ordinary onion) peeled and chopped

2 leeks, trimmed, washed, and sliced finely

300g OR 10½oz mixed root vegetables, washed, peeled if not organic, and diced finely

1.2 litres OR 40fl oz vegetable stock (*see* page 13)

100g OR 3½ oz long-grain rice

100g OR 3½ oz peas, fresh or frozen

100g OR 3½ oz green beans, cut into 2cm OR ¾-inch slices

Heat the olive oil and gently sweat the onions and leeks for five minutes.

Add the diced vegetables. Stir until thoroughly coated with oil.

Pour in the stock and rice and simmer for fifteen minutes.

Add the peas and beans and continue simmering until tender.

For protection against colds and flu …

Root vegetables offer a **mineral boost**

Beans and **peas** provide natural **plant hormones**

Leeks add protective **phytochemicals**

Cabbage soup with gammon

Cabbage has been the medicine of the poor since a pot was first hung over a fire in prehistoric times. Of all the vegetables, cabbage and its relatives must be regarded as among the most important for their medicinal value. This soup also provides a good dose of protein from the gammon and immune-enhancing carotenoids from the vegetable stock.

300g OR 10½ oz gammon (or more for a very robust soup), fat removed

4 tablespoons extra-virgin olive oil

2 red onions, peeled and finely chopped

1.5 litres OR 55fl oz vegetable stock (*see* page 13)

300g OR 10½ oz potatoes, peeled and cubed

500g OR 1 lb 2oz organic Savoy cabbage, finely shredded

200g OR 7oz noodles or spaghettini

Cube the gammon, dry-fry, and reserve.

Heat the oil.

Sweat the onions in the oil.

Add the stock and the potatoes and simmer until the potatoes are just tender.

Whiz in a food processor or blender until smooth.

Return to the pan and bring back to a simmer.

Add the cabbage and cook for five minutes.

Stir in the noodles or spaghettini and the gammon and continue cooking for about three to four minutes until the pasta or noodles are *al dente*.

Serve with beetroot floaters (*see* page 131).

For prevention and protection …

Cabbage is rich in **antibacterial sulphur** and cancer-fighting **thiocynates**

Potatoes provide **vitamin C**

Chicken, chilli, chard, and noodles

You'll obtain plenty of health benefits here from the traditional immune-strengthening properties of chicken soup. In addition to the health-promoting benefits of chard and chilli, the egg noodles provide a little iron and easily absorbed energy – always important in the body's fight against infection.

3 tablespoons extra-virgin olive oil

1 large onion, peeled and very finely chopped

1 medium red chilli, seeds removed, very finely chopped

1.2 litres OR 40fl oz chicken stock (*see* page 15)

150g OR 5½ oz chard, stalks torn from the leaves

250g OR 9oz egg noodles

Heat the olive oil and sweat the onion and chilli gently for five minutes.

Add the stock, bring to the boil, turn down the heat, and simmer for ten minutes.

Strain into a clean saucepan.

Slice the chard stalks very finely, add to the pan, and simmer for ten minutes.

Tear the chard leaves roughly and add to the pan with the noodles.

Simmer until tender – usually not more than three minutes.

To aid in the fight against infection …

Chard is an amazing source of
betacarotenes

Chillies contain **capsaicin,**

which stimulates the circulation

Duck soup with prunes

Duck, like chicken, is a delicious source of a whole host of vitamins and minerals. The unusual addition of prunes makes this soup an extremely high source of protective antioxidants, and their slight sweetness is balanced by the parsley, thyme, and rosemary, which also provide beneficial essential oils.

1 cooked duck carcass, some flesh still attached, but with all the skin and visible fat removed

2 bay leaves

Bouquet garni: 3 sprigs each parsley, thyme, and rosemary, tied together with string, or a good commercial bouquet garni bag

1 large onion, peeled and finely chopped

2 large carrots, trimmed and peeled if not organic, coarsely chopped

2 stalks of celery, coarsely chopped

10 whole peppercorns

Up to 1.5 litres OR 55fl oz of vegetable stock (*see* page 13)

200g OR 7oz prunes, stoned (or dried apricots, if preferred)

Put all the ingredients except the prunes into a large saucepan.

Bring to the boil and simmer for an hour.

Strain into a bowl.

Set aside the duck. Discard the bouquet garni and push some of the vegetables through a sieve into the stock, depending on how thick you like the soup. Add vegetable stock at this stage to give the quantity and texture you prefer.

When the duck is cool enough to handle, scrape off the remaining meat and add to the stock.

Chop or snip the prunes (or apricots) into peanut-sized pieces.

Add to the pan and simmer gently for twenty minutes.

To fortify general immunity …

Duck is rich in body-building

protein, protective **enzymes,** and **B vitamins**

Bay leaves provide

cineole and **laurenolide,**

essential oils which fight respiratory infections

Circul

ation
Soups

Soups are often associated with the chilly, damp, dark, and depressing days of winter, when the image of a steaming bowl of hot broth brings much-needed warmth to icy hands and feet. In fact, the physical effect of soup has far more to do with its ingredients than with the temperature of the soup itself.

Naturally, there is a powerful psychological benefit to be gained from cupping your hands around a steaming bowl of hot goodness, but this can't be relied upon to set the blood coursing through your veins. Many people need a circulation boost in *all* weathers – not just in winter. While the capillaries – the tiniest blood vessels at the very end of the circulatory system – naturally constrict in cold weather to conserve body heat, people who suffer from poor circulation endure cool extremities all year round. The problem is more common in women than men, even when the former are in otherwise perfect health.

As irritating as these milder cases are, those who suffer from an illness called Raynaud's disease have more severe circulatory problems. This condition shuts down the blood supply to the outer parts of the body; although it most commonly affects the hands and fingers, it can also occur in the feet, toes, nose, and even the ears. What triggers the onset of Raynaud's is hard to predict. Simple factors, such as stepping into an air-conditioned room on a hot summer's day, can cause the fingers to go parchment white and become "dead-feeling" and painful. Eventually, they may turn blue or black, and when the blood finally begins to flow again, the pain becomes even more unbearable. Fortunately, help is at hand. Whether it's cold weather, poor circulation, Raynaud's disease or any other circulatory problem, the circulation soups in this chapter will come to the rescue. Just as in the previous chapter, the recipes here employ the benefits of onions, leeks, and garlic, all of which help improve blood-flow. Then there are the advantages of beetroot, used for centuries in eastern Europe as a traditional remedy to improve the quality of blood and its circulation. Special emphasis is also given to a group of nutrients called bioflavonoids, which are vital for maintaining the health and integrity of blood-vessel walls. One of the richest sources of these natural protectors is cherries. And yes, you *can* make soup from cherries – just *see* page 44.

Spices are renowned for the dramatic way in which they stimulate the circulation; who hasn't broken into a sweat, for example, halfway through a bowl of curry or chilli con carne? Ginger, curry mixtures, chilli, horseradish, mustard seeds, and all other hot spices are used in these recipes to help improve the way blood moves around the body.

Two factors that can severely affect circulation are the clotting tendency of blood and high levels of cholesterol. Cholesterol is deposited on the inside of the artery walls, which results in the narrowing of these vessels, making it more difficult for the blood to get through. Major ingredients that specifically target both these problems are the mono-unsaturated fats in olive oil, natural phytochemicals in garlic, onions, and leeks, and the soluble fibre in oats, lentils, and root vegetables. All of these work to eliminate cholesterol from the body and lower the risk of fatty deposits in the arteries, as well as reducing the stickiness of the blood so that it flows more easily.

Winter or summer, the benefits of these delicious soups will help maintain the efficiency and effectiveness of your body's circulation. The bonus is that they're all also extremely rich in the vital nutrients that contribute to your general health – protecting you against many other diseases at the same time.

Spiced lentil soup

In this soup, spices come into their own, working together to get your circulation buzzing. Add B vitamins and good fibre from the lentils, and calcium, phosphorus, and magnesium from the coconut milk, and you have an effective, delicious, and satisfying dish for circulatory health.

3 tablespoons extra-virgin olive oil

1 medium onion, peeled and finely sliced

1 clove garlic, peeled and finely chopped

2.5cm OR 1 inch fresh ginger root, peeled and finely grated

1 tablespoon coriander seed, crushed well

1 tablespoon allspice

1 teaspoon chilli powder

700ml OR 25fl oz vegetable stock (*see* page 13)

1 x 400ml OR 14fl oz can of coconut milk

150g OR 5½oz green lentils

Heat the olive oil in a large saucepan.

Stir in the onion and sweat gently for five minutes.

Add the garlic and ginger and continue sweating for four minutes.

Stir in the coriander, allspice, and chilli powder and cook, stirring continuously, for three minutes.

Add the stock and coconut milk and bring to a simmer.

Stir in the lentils and continue to simmer for about thirty minutes.

To spice up your blood-flow …

Ginger provides **gingeroles,**
essential oils that dilate blood vessels

Chilli adds **capsaicin** for stimulating warmth

Curried parsnip and vegetable soup

Putting parsnips together with stimulating spices such as curry produces a soup that is seriously good for your circulation. Adding beans and peas increases the fibre content and supplies beneficial protein, while the crème fraîche gives it a wonderfully creamy texture and supplies calcium, too.

4 tablespoons extra-virgin olive oil

1 large onion, peeled and finely chopped

1 heaped tablespoon curry powder

2 level tablespoons flour

2 medium parsnips (about 500g OR 1 lb 2oz) washed, peeled, and diced

1.2 litres OR 40fl oz vegetable stock (*see* page 13)

200ml OR 7fl oz crème fraîche

100g OR 3½oz French beans, trimmed and cut into 2.5cm OR 1-inch fingers

100g OR 3½oz peas, fresh or frozen

Heat the olive oil and gently sweat the onions for ten minutes.

Remove from the heat and stir in the curry powder and flour.

Return to the heat and cook, stirring continuously, for three minutes.

Add the diced parsnips and stir for two more minutes.

Pour in the stock and bring to the boil.

Simmer for twenty minutes, or until the parsnips are tender.

Liquidize the mixture, return to the pan, and bring back to a simmer.

Stir in the crème fraîche.

Add the beans and peas and cook for another seven minutes.

To keep blood flowing freely …

Parsnips are rich in
minerals and **fibre**

Beans and **peas** supply beneficial
plant hormones

Ginger, leek, and carrot soup

The leek is a member of the *Allium* genus of plants and, just like its onion and garlic relatives, it is a rich source of natural sulphur-based chemicals that improve the circulation. This recipe provides a triple boost from all three. As an extra circulatory bonus, there's plenty of ginger as well.

3 teaspoons extra-virgin olive oil

1 large red onion, peeled and finely sliced

3 plump cloves of garlic, peeled and finely chopped

3 large leeks, trimmed, washed, and finely chopped

2.5cm OR 1 inch fresh root ginger, peeled and grated

1kg OR 2 lb 4oz carrots, trimmed and peeled if not organic, finely diced

1.2 litres OR 40fl oz vegetable stock (*see* page 13)

Heat the olive oil in a large saucepan.

Add the onion, garlic, leeks, and ginger and sweat gently for ten minutes.

Drop in the carrot cubes and stir until covered with the oil mixture.

Pour in the stock and bring to the boil.

Turn down the heat and simmer until the carrots are tender – about twenty minutes.

Liquidize in a food processor or blender.

Pour through a fine sieve, being careful to remove any unliquidized ginger.

NOTE: this soup is delicious hot or cold. If you're in a rush, use carrot or vegetable juice instead of fresh carrots. You could also combine orange with carrot juice and use commercially produced crushed ginger. This puts up the price, but remember: this recipe makes enough to last two or three days.

For reducing blood pressure …

Leeks contain

phytochemicals

that help lower cholesterol, which keeps blood-pressure levels down

Beetroot soup

Throughout eastern Europe, beetroot is renowned for its blood- and circulation-boosting properties. Served as soup or juice, this vegetable has been used in the treatment of anaemia, poor circulation, and even leukaemia. In this recipe, it is combined with carrots and lemon juice to provide a refreshing, nourishing soup for healthy blood.

1kg OR 2 lb 4oz fresh, raw beetroot (pickled ones are not suitable)

2 large carrots, trimmed and peeled if not organic

1 clove garlic, peeled

1 medium white onion, peeled

5 tablespoons extra-virgin olive oil

1.5 litres OR 55fl oz vegetable stock (*see* page 13)

Juice of 1 lemon

400ml OR 14fl oz yoghurt

Grate the beetroot, carrots, onion, and garlic, or chop them in a food processor.

Heat the oil in a large saucepan. Add the vegetables and sweat gently for ten minutes.

Add the stock and simmer, covered, for forty minutes.

Strain into a clean saucepan and bring back to a simmer.

Stir the lemon juice into the yoghurt.

Serve the soup with a swirl of the yoghurt and lemon mixture on top and beetroot floaters (*see* page 131). Alternatively, serve cold, substituting white seedless grapes for the yoghurt and lemon mixture.

For a traditional circulation treatment …

Beetroot is rich in **iron,** which helps prevent anaemia

Carrots supply **betacarotene** to protect capillaries

Vitamin C in lemons prevents damage to artery walls

Oatmeal and broccoli soup

As well as being a healthy breakfast food in the form of porridge, oats are a versatile ingredient and can be used to delicious advantage in many other ways. In this unusual soup, they're combined with broccoli to make a surprisingly light and delicate dish that offers huge health benefits.

2 tablespoons extra-virgin olive oil

6 spring onions, finely chopped

600g OR 1 lb 5oz broccoli florets, washed, trimmed, and halved if very large

75g OR 2³/₄ oz oatmeal

750ml OR 27fl oz semi-skimmed milk

750ml OR 27fl oz vegetable stock (*see* page 13)

sea salt and black pepper

4 tablespoons yoghurt

A generous bunch of chives, finely snipped

Heat the oil on a low heat and sweat the onions until soft – about five minutes.

Add the broccoli and continue heating gently, stirring continuously, for three more minutes.

Mix in the oatmeal and continue cooking for four minutes, still stirring.

Pour in the milk and stock, cover, and simmer for ten minutes; season to taste.

Serve with a spoonful of yoghurt in each bowl.

Scatter with the chives or with herb croutons (*see* page 128).

NOTE: top each dish with a chive flower for a more sophisticated look.

To protect the heart …

Oats are rich in
B vitamins and soluble fibre

Broccoli supplies
vitamin C and betacarotene
which protect the heart and help prevent cancer

Oxtail soup

In spite of the worries about BSE, I can't recommend this robust, hearty soup strongly enough. Make sure that you buy organic oxtail; there hasn't been a single case of BSE on a certified organic farm in the UK. Add the stimulating spices in Worcestershire or Tabasco sauce, and this soup is sure to warm the very cockles of your heart.

About 8 x 2.5cm OR 1-inch chunks of oxtail

1 large cupful of flour, seasoned with plenty of black pepper and a little sea salt

5 tablespoons extra-virgin olive oil

1 large onion, peeled and coarsely chopped

2 cloves of garlic, peeled and finely chopped

1 large carrot, trimmed and peeled if not organic, diced very finely

1 medium turnip, trimmed, peeled, and finely diced

Half a large swede, peeled and finely diced

1.5 litres OR 55fl oz beef stock (*see* page 17)

3 tablespoons tomato purée

2 teaspoons Worcestershire OR Tabasco sauce

2 bay leaves

1 generous handful of parsley, finely chopped

Trim as much fat as possible off the oxtail.

Coat the meat in seasoned flour and set aside.

In a large saucepan, heat the olive oil and gently sweat the vegetables for ten minutes, stirring continuously.

In another pan, sear the seasoned oxtail in a little more oil.

Add the meat to the saucepan.

Pour in the stock and add the tomato purée and Worcestershire or Tabasco sauce and bay leaves.

Simmer gently for fifty minutes, or until the meat is tender.

Remove the bay leaves.

Serve scattered with parsley, either with the oxtail still intact or with the bone removed.

NOTE: for a more sustaining main meal, add baby potatoes just as the soup comes to a simmer.

To revitalize the circulatory system …

Oxtail is bursting with
B vitamins and iron for healthy blood

Turnips, swede, and carrot provide
betacarotene and minerals
for good circulation

Sweet cherry soup

It's easy to think of cherries as simply one of those delicious summer treats, but they're much more than that. Ripe, plump cherries are a storehouse of circulation-boosting nutrients. Combined with an extra dose of vitamin C from the cranberry juice, this soup will benefit anyone's circulatory system.

1kg OR 2 lbs 4oz cherries, weighed when stoned

250ml OR 9fl oz cranberry juice

500ml OR 18fl oz water

1 glass sweet white wine, such as Muscat de Beaumes-de-Venise or the less expensive Monbazillac

1 level tablespoon arrowroot

4 sprigs mint

Blend the cherries in a food processor or blender and sieve to remove the skins.

Put the pulp into a large pan with the cranberry juice, water, and wine and bring slowly to the boil, stirring well.

Stir the arrowroot into two more tablespoons of water and mix thoroughly.

Pour the arrowroot mixture into the fruit stock and stir continuously until slightly thickened.

Serve garnished with the sprigs of mint.

NOTE: this soup is delicious warm or cold. You can make it with other summer fruits, particularly strawberries, and substitute the wine with extra fruit juice if you're serving children.

For a circulatory boost …

Cherries are rich in
bioflavonoids and **vitamin C**

both of which support healthy blood

Skin-
rev

iving

Soups

The eyes may be the mirrors of the soul, but as many modern doctors now admit, your skin is an accurate mirror of your eating habits. Of course, no food or special diet is a cure for every skin condition.

But no matter what problem you're having, the food you eat can help it to improve, or conversely, can aggravate things so much that even a minor skin disorder rapidly degenerates into a catastrophe – which can plunge you into despair, especially if you're an already image-conscious teenager. For some sufferers, the psychological ramifications of acne, eczema, and psoriasis can be so profound that they radically alter their personality. For both men and women, any condition perceived as being embarrassing, disfiguring or abnormal can lead to withdrawal from social activities, isolation, lack of achievement at school, college or work – and possibly even clinical depression.

This triggers an inevitable vicious circle: "My acne is bad; I'm unattractive; I'm embarrassed; I won't go out with my friends; I'm ugly; I don't have any friends; I'm miserable; I deserve three doughnuts, a slab of chocolate, and a bottle of wine; I wake up feeling sick; I've got a hangover; my acne is worse; I'm more depressed; I'll have more chocolate and wine…".

OK, so this is an extreme scenario, but believe me, it does happen. I've seen it in so many of my patients. It doesn't matter what age you are or the circumstances in which you live, any skin problem can be a disaster. This is one situation in which molehills often turn into mountains. The spot on your nose on the day of an important interview or your first date suddenly seems the size of a golf ball. That patch of grey, flaky eczema under your eyes is bound to flare up the day before your wedding. And halfway through the meal with your prospective in-laws, you just know that you'll come out in hives. That's why this chapter on skin-reviving soups has been included: to take the strain out of such "personal appearances". Not only do these soups help you over the hurdles as they appear, but by including these recipes regularly in your normal weekly eating plan, you'll be doing everything you can to nourish, heal, protect, and revitalize your skin. If you really want to keep those zits at bay, then my advice is to eat soup.

It's certainly a cheaper (and healthier) option than covering yourself with expensive facial products, many of which do nothing more than moisturize the skin. The most important of the skin nutrients abound in some of the most inexpensive, simple, and easy-to-cook foods. Betacarotene, for example, is a major ingredient in carrots, pumpkins, sweet potatoes, and sweetcorn, none of which will make a dent in your budget. Yet this nutrient is one of the best friends your skin has. The stuff that gives these vegetables their colour also functions as a protective antioxidant – meaning it's anti-ageing as well.

What's more, all root vegetables are rich in minerals, particularly skin-friendly zinc. The vitamin C from oranges, potatoes, and leeks is also essential for natural resistance to a wide range of infections. In addition, the sulphur compounds present in onions, leeks, chives, spring onions, and garlic are powerful weapons in your skin's fight against bacterial and fungal infections. When it comes to conditions such as dry skin, eczema, and psoriasis, the healing effects of vitamin E – found in olive oil, almonds, and egg yolks – are second to none. Finally, the natural anti-inflammatory properties of the essential oil known as gingerol, found in fresh ginger, can help take the sting out of most skin disorders.

Of course, these soups are good for more than giving your skin the vital bloom and glowing texture it deserves. Like most recipes in this book, these skin-reviving soups all look good, taste great, and will help the rest of your body feel good into the bargain.

Iced fennel soup

The familiar, subtle, and delicate taste of Florence fennel comes from its high content of essential oils. These can help reduce the amount of a fatty substance known as sebum, which is excreted by the skin; that reduction, in turn, helps prevent acne.

2 large bulbs of Florence fennel, preferably with fronds

500g OR 1 lb 2oz small new potatoes

1 litre OR 35fl oz vegetable stock (*see* page 13)

2 cloves

300ml OR 10fl oz milk

Half a teaspoon grated nutmeg

Wash and roughly chop the fennel bulbs, but keep the fronds for later.

Wash but don't peel the potatoes.

Put the fennel bulbs and potatoes in the stock with the cloves. Simmer for twenty minutes.

Remove from the heat and discard the cloves.

Liquidize the mixture, then return to the heat and add the milk.

Transfer to a tureen and, when cool enough, put into the fridge.

In the meantime, sprinkle the reserved fennel fronds into an ice-cube tray. Fill with water and freeze.

Serve the soup with a couple of ice-cubes in each dish and a sprinkle of nutmeg on top.

To soothe irritated skin …

Fennel bulbs are rich in

fenchone, a gentle liver stimulant that improves the breakdown, digestion, and elimination of dietary fats

Carrot and almond cream

Using carrots to combat skin problems shouldn't be a surprise. Of all the root vegetables, they're the best-designed to help with any skin disorder, owing to their high content of healing phytochemicals. Adding almonds gives this soup a hefty boost of minerals, leeks provide antibacterial sulphur compounds, while egg yolks are a rich source of iron and vitamin E – both vital for supple, smooth skin.

3 tablespoons extra-virgin olive oil

1 large leek, trimmed, washed, and finely sliced

1.2 litres or 40fl oz vegetable stock (*see* page 13)

4 large carrots, trimmed and peeled if not organic, sliced

100g or 3½oz ground almonds

250ml or 9fl oz double cream

2 egg yolks

In a large saucepan, heat the oil and sweat the leek gently for about five minutes.

Add the stock, carrots, and ground almonds and simmer until the vegetables are tender – around ten to fifteen minutes.

Whisk together the cream and egg yolks.

Liquidize the carrot and almond mixture. Pour into the cream and egg yolks, whisking or stirring thoroughly.

Re-heat gently.

For a very finely textured soup, push through a sieve, or strain through kitchen muslin at this stage (I never bother).

Serve with Emmental croutons (*see* page 128).

For skin nourishment and health …

Carrots are packed with
betacarotene, essential for healthy skin

Almonds supply **zinc** and **selenium**
to nourish the skin

Sweet potato and garlic soup

Britain must be one of the best places in the world to live if you're a foodie. Its multi-cultural society means that a wide choice of foods from every part of the world can be found in British corner shops, street markets, and supermarkets. One of the nicest and healthiest of these ethnic imports is the sweet potato, which, thanks to its massive content of betacarotene, is great skin food however you eat it.

2 bulbs of garlic

750g OR 1 lb 10oz sweet potatoes, peeled and cubed

1.5 litres OR 55fl oz vegetable stock (see page 13)

Cut the tops off the garlic bulbs, but don't peel them. Wrap them in foil and roast at 200°C OR 400°F OR gas mark 6 for fiften to twenty minutes, depending on size.

Meanwhile, simmer the sweet potatoes in the stock and whiz until smooth using a food processor or blender.

Cool the garlic until it's comfortable to handle, then squeeze out the pulp.

Put the sweet potato mixture back on the heat.

Add the garlic pulp and whisk thoroughly.

Serve garnished with onion floaters (see page 131).

NOTE: for an extra-special touch, sprinkle chive or garlic flowers on top.

To prevent dry skin and infection …

Sweet potatoes provide vital
betacarotene and **vitamin E** to help dry, fragile skin

Garlic helps prevent fungal infections and acne

Spicy carrot and orange soup

This quick and easy soup is very inexpensive, full of nutrients, and looks spectacular served in white bowls as a starter for a dinner party. Its powerhouse of healing skin essentials and terrific taste make it ideal in winter or summer, so serve it all year round to revitalize your complexion.

4 tablespoons extra-virgin olive oil

1 large onion, peeled and finely chopped

2.5cm OR 1 inch fresh ginger root, peeled and grated

900g OR 2 lb carrots, trimmed and peeled if not organic, sliced

1.5 litres OR 55fl oz water

500ml OR 18fl oz fresh orange juice

4 tablespoons single cream

Heat the oil in a large saucepan, and sweat the onion and ginger gently until soft.

Add the carrots to the pan and coat with the oil.

Pour in the water and orange juice and simmer until the carrots are tender – usually ten to fifteen minutes, depending on how finely they're sliced.

Liquidize or blend until smooth.

Pour into bowls and serve with swirls of cream on top.

For a good dose of skin protection …

Olive oil is rich in essential **vitamin E**

Carrots supply vital **betacarotene**

Orange juice provides immune-boosting **vitamin C**

Sweetcorn and smoked haddock chowder

The Scottish tradition of making delicious soup from smoked haddock is centuries old. Haddock is a rich source of perfect protein without saturated fat, and it also supplies significant amounts of essential minerals. What's more, when combined with sweetcorn and healing herbs, it makes a hearty, healthy chowder.

600g OR 1 lb 5oz undyed, naturally smoked haddock, skinned, all bones removed

1 litre OR 35fl oz milk

4 bay leaves

2 sprigs each of parsley, dill, sage, and thyme, tied firmly together with string

6 spring onions, trimmed and finely sliced

250ml OR 9fl oz fish stock (see page 14)

400g OR 14oz sweetcorn, preferably fresh from the cob, but canned or frozen will do

100ml OR 3½ fl oz single cream

Put the smoked haddock into the milk.

Add the bay leaves, herbs, and onions.

Simmer for ten minutes and leave to cool.

Remove the bay leaves and herbs.

Strain the fish from the milk, reserving both.

Put the stock and the milk into a large pan.

Add the sweetcorn and simmer for five minutes.

Flake the fish and add to the pan with the cream.

Serve warm with a spoonful of rouille (*see* page 129) or herb croutons (*see* page 128) on top.

To cleanse the skin …

Haddock is rich in **iodine,** which helps regulate the thyroid gland

Sweetcorn provides essential **vitamin A**

Sage and **thyme** offer cleansing, **antiseptic essential oils**

Pumpkin soup with nasturtium flowers

How sad that the wonderful flavour and nutritional value of pumpkins only emerges for Halloween – and even then, they're wasted as decorative jack-o'-lanterns. Yet pumpkins are perfect as a healthy alternative to stodgier winter foods, and in this soup they help counteract the dehydrating effects of central heating. Topped with nasturtium flowers, this is one dish that looks as delicious as it tastes.

2 large, white onions, peeled and finely chopped

2 cloves of garlic, peeled and finely chopped

2 tablespoons extra-virgin olive oil

25g OR 1oz unsalted butter

3 teaspoons curry powder or paste

1 litre OR 35fl oz vegetable stock (*see* page 13)

1kg OR 1 lb 4oz pumpkin (or squash or courgettes) deseeded, peeled, and cubed

4 tablespoons crème fraîche

4 nasturtium flowers (use chive flowers if unavailable)

Sweat the onions and garlic gently in the oil and butter.

Add the curry powder or paste and cook for two minutes, stirring continuously.

Pour in the vegetable stock and bring to a boil.

Add the pumpkin to the stock.

Simmer until the vegetables are just tender.

Liquidize in a food processor or blender.

Stir in the crème fraîche and mix thoroughly.

Serve with nasturtium flowers or courgette floaters (*see* page 131) on top.

To lift and rejuvenate the complexion …

Pumpkin gives a boost of
betacarotene and folic acid

Nasturtium flowers are rich in
antibacterial mustard oils

Sex

y Soups

It's extraordinary that with increasing media focus on sex, there appears to be a directly proportional growth in sexual problems. As strange as it seems, the more people see of it in the cinema, on television, and in print, the less they seem able to "perform" in their own bedrooms.

While it's true that some sexual problems have a psychological root, the percentage of people, both men and women, whose physical relationships are less than satisfactory is now known to be far greater than was previously thought. Male impotence, loss of libido in both sexes, fertility problems, and a marked increase in decline in women's arousal and satisfaction are all problems faced by many otherwise happy and compatible couples.

From a medical point of view, it is known that a range of underlying conditions can affect sexual performance and enjoyment. High blood pressure, raised cholesterol levels, diabetes, heart disease, circulatory difficulties, neurological disorders, and even simple diseases of wear and tear such as osteo-arthritis can all interfere with the ability to perform or enjoy everyday sexual relationships. To make matters worse, the medication prescribed for some of these conditions can also have a devastating effect on libido and erectile function.

But the trouble doesn't stop there. The single largest factor in this equation is food: specifically, a regular, long-term intake of food that supplies only marginal amounts of some of the key sexually essential ingredients. Over fifty per cent of women attending fertility clinics have been on some form of drastic weight-loss diet in the twelve months prior to their visit. Sperm counts in British men have halved in the last three decades. This rise in sexual problems has gone hand in hand with a decreasing nutritional content in food caused by intensive farming, and with pollution by insecticides, pesticides, and hormone-disrupting chemicals. It has been compounded by a rising consumption of high-fat, high-salt, and high-sugar foods.

Scientists may poke fun at the idea of aphrodisiac foods, but many ingredients in the following recipes have been used for centuries. The fact is that nutrients such as zinc, selenium, iron, iodine, and vitamins A, C, and E all play a well-researched part in the ability to achieve and maintain satisfaction through successful sexual activity. Worryingly, these are the very nutrients that have declined most in the average British diet.

That is why they are used liberally in "Sexy Soups". The recipes in this chapter aren't just designed to give your sex life a boost; they've been created to taste good, look appealing, and provide the sensations of sensuality that are essential for loving sexuality. Prawns, for example, are rich in zinc: vital for sperm formation. When married with the heady aroma of lemon grass and the circulatory booster of coriander, they create a stimulating sweet-and-sour soup (*see* page 66). Given their vitamin E and iron content, it is no coincidence that eggs are a universal symbol of fertility; they're featured on page 62. The combination of yoghurt, mint, and garlic has a long aphrodisiacal tradition in folklore. They're used on page 64 in a fabulous chilled soup that sets the scene for a night of consuming passion.

Although traditionally thought to be a great male aphrodisiac because of their extremely high zinc content, molluscs contain essential fatty acids that can have the same effect on women. One large bowl of Mussel chowder (*see* page 70) shared intimately between lovers is all you need. Equally dramatic (and for similar reasons) is the combination of oysters with that legendary aphrodisiac vegetable, asparagus (*see* page 68).

Of course, you don't have to have performance problems to take advantage of sexy soups. Whatever the reason, my advice is the same: eat, drink, and be sexy.

Vegetable broth with poached egg

Eggs are the ultimate symbol of fertility. Poached gently in this nutrient-rich stock, they provide much-needed essential ingredients for a night of consuming passion.

1.5 litres OR 55fl oz vegetable stock (*see* page 13 – no stock cubes allowed here)

2 large carrots, trimmed and peeled if not organic, finely diced

1 small turnip, finely diced

1 large handful of whole fresh herbs, such as sage, thyme, rosemary, and bay leaves

4 organic eggs

8 whole sprigs of flat-leaf parsley

In a large saucepan, bring the stock to simmering point. Add the vegetables and herbs, and boil briskly until reduced by about a quarter – usually fifteen minutes.

Strain out the herbs and vegetables, then pour the broth back into the pan.

Place the eggs – still in their shells – in the simmering stock for about twenty seconds (this holds the egg whites together).

Crack the eggs and poach carefully in the stock until just set – about four minutes.

Serve the soup with the eggs floating on top and garnished with the parsley leaves.

NOTE: you can make this soup several hours before serving. Prepare to the stage at which the eggs have poached, remove them, and place in cold water in the fridge. When ready to serve, put them into the simmering stock for one minute and they'll warm up wonderfully.

For a boost of sensual nutrients …

Eggs supply

protein, iron and **vitamin E**

all vital to healthy sexual performance

Chilled yoghurt and cucumber soup

Throughout Greece and the Middle East, tzatziki is renowned as a potent aphrodisiac. This soup combines the traditional ingredients of yoghurt, mint, and garlic with a lavish helping of tomato juice.

1 large or 2 small cucumbers, peeled and deseeded

500ml OR 18fl oz yoghurt, preferably live and "bio"

300ml OR 10fl oz tomato juice

1 large clove of garlic, peeled and finely chopped

1 litre OR 35fl oz cold vegetable stock (*see* page 13)

1 large bunch of fresh mint, woody stems removed, finely chopped

1 teaspoon Worcestershire sauce

Slice the cucumber finely and put in layers in a colander, covering each layer with a sprinkle of salt. Leave for an hour to allow the excess moisture to run out.

Meanwhile, mix together the yoghurt, tomato juice, garlic, stock, and most of the mint.

Tip the cucumber onto a clean tea towel and squeeze out the rest of the moisture. If necessary, chop gently again.

Stir the cucumber into the yoghurt mixture.

Serve with a dash of Worcestershire sauce in each bowl and scatter with the rest of the mint.

For male sexual health …

Tomatoes are rich in **lycopene,** which is essential for the health of the prostate gland

Lettuce, mint, and pea soup

You may find it hard to think of pea soup as sexy – but believe me, this one is. Its wonderfully fresh colour conveys a hint of nature and new beginnings. What few people know is that lettuce also contains some amazing mood-enhancing chemicals; in fact, the ancient Greeks used the sap from the cut stems of wild lettuce to make a sleep- and dream-inducing medicine. I don't need to tell you what sort of dreams they were ….

70g OR 2½ oz unsalted butter

1 large onion, peeled and finely chopped

1 large iceberg lettuce, finely chopped

1 heaped tablespoon flour

1.2 litres OR 40fl oz chicken OR vegetable stock (*see* page 15 or 13)

500g OR 1 lb 2oz peas (frozen will do)

1 large bunch of mint, woody stems removed, finely chopped

About 280ml OR 10fl oz sour cream

In a large saucepan, melt the butter over a low heat and gently sweat the onion for five minutes.

Add the lettuce and stir until covered with the butter mixture.

Stir in the flour and cook gently for three to four minutes.

Add the stock and bring to the boil.

Reduce the heat. Add the peas and most of the mint and simmer until the peas are tender.

Serve with a large spoonful of sour cream on top and scattered with the rest of the mint.

To ensure female sexual health …

Peas are rich in

natural plant hormones

that contribute to female sexuality

Thai sweet-and-sour soup

This deliciously light soup is a delight for all the senses. By combining prawns with the tang of coriander (which has a long tradition in Asia as an aphrodisiac) and the heady, aromatic oils in lemon grass, you've got a sure-fire winner for a night of passion.

1 litre OR **35fl oz fish stock** (*see* page 14)

1 x 5-cm OR **2-inch stalk of lemon grass**

2 limes

2 tablespoons runny honey (preferably organic)

1 handful of chopped coriander leaves, plus four whole, tender sprigs

500g OR **1 lb 2oz prawns, shelled**

In a large saucepan, warm the stock over a low heat.

Crush the lemon grass thoroughly.

Juice the limes. Mix the juice with the honey and lemon grass and heat gently with half the stock for five minutes.

Remove the lemon grass and pour the honey mixture into the rest of the stock, along with the chopped coriander.

Simmer for two minutes, stirring continuously.

Add the prawns and poach gently for five minutes.

Serve sprinkled with the reserved coriander leaves.

To promote good sexual function …

Prawns are rich in

zinc, vital for the formation of sperm

and **essential fatty acids** that help maintain fertility

Asparagus soup

Of all vegetables, asparagus is regarded as the most potent aphrodisiac, with celery following a pretty close second. Asparagus is one of the oldest of cultivated vegetables and has been grown as food for more than 6,000 years. Adding oysters, the most potent of all the aphrodisiac foods, guarantees that this will be the sexiest soup you've ever tasted.

50g OR 1³/₄oz unsalted butter

4 large spring onions, trimmed and finely sliced

2 stalks of celery, very finely sliced

3 level tablespoons flour

1.2 litres OR 40fl oz vegetable stock (*see* page 13)

500g OR 1 lb 2oz (trimmed weight) fresh asparagus (use canned only if you must)

200ml OR 7fl oz live bio-yoghurt

Half a handful of fresh tarragon stems, left whole

4 oysters (the flat, native variety if possible)

In a large saucepan, melt the butter until soft.

Sweat the spring onions and celery gently in the butter for about five minutes.

Mix in the flour and stir until the vegetables are well-coated.

Pour in the stock and add the asparagus.

Bring to the boil, then simmer until the asparagus is tender – about eight minutes if fresh, or just to boiling point if using canned.

Remove eight asparagus pieces and set aside.

Liquidize or blend until smooth. Return to the rinsed saucepan.

Add the yoghurt and whisk thoroughly.

Tip in the reserved asparagus pieces and sprigs of tarragon and heat to a simmer.

Serve with the oysters floating on top.

For an aphrodisiac boost …

Asparagus contains plant hormones called

asparagosides,

which balance hormones and are mildly diuretic

Oysters are rich in zinc, which is vital for sexual function

Game soup

This is just the soup to get you in the mood for the game of love. Although it might sound rich and heavy, it's actually a very delicate and nourishing broth that is extremely low in fat, very rich in vital sexual nutrients, and enhanced by the sensual aromatic oils in rosemary, sage, and thyme. All game birds, such as wild duck, pheasant, partridge or grouse, are delicious in roasts or in casseroles and stews. With this recipe, you can enjoy eating them one day and having the soup the next.

**Cooked game carcasses:
1 duck or pheasant, 2 pigeons or other smaller birds, or a combination**

2 litres OR 75fl oz water

1 large onion, peeled and finely chopped

1 large leek, washed and coarsely chopped

2 large stalks of celery, chopped

1 large sprig of rosemary

Half a large bunch of parsley

1 large sprig of sage

2 large sprigs of thyme

3 bay leaves

About 200g OR 7oz of any root vegetables, cut into julienne strips

Half a wine glass of port

Put the carcass (or carcasses) into a large saucepan; cover with the water.

Bring to the boil and simmer for about an hour.

Add the onion, leek, celery, and herbs.

Bring back to the boil and simmer for forty minutes.

Strain through kitchen muslin or a sieve.

Leave to cool until the fat rises to the top.

Skim off any fat.

Add the julienne vegetables and simmer until just tender.

Tip in the port and serve.

To supply fortifying essential nutrients …

Game birds provide

B vitamins, natural enzymes, and minerals

which all promote sexual function and a healthy heart

Mussel chowder

All molluscs are great aphrodisiac foods; they're blessed with this reputation wherever they're eaten. There are as many variations of this recipe as there are zip codes in America, where the famous New England chowder is made with clams. My version uses mussels, which gain added flavour from the bacon.

4 tablespoons extra-virgin olive oil

4 thin slices of unsmoked back bacon, cut into strips

2 large stalks of celery, very finely chopped

3 large spring onions

2 small potatoes, peeled and finely diced

1 litre OR 35fl oz fish stock (*see* page 14)

3 large sprigs of tarragon

3 large sprigs each of parsley, dill, and tarragon, tied together with string

3 bay leaves

About 1.5kg OR 5lb 5oz mussels

2 glasses dry white wine

1 large handful of finely chopped parsley

In a large saucepan, heat half the oil on a low heat and sauté the bacon until crisp. Remove the bacon and set aside.

Add the rest of the oil and tip in the celery, spring onions, and potatoes. Stir to coat thoroughly with the oil and cook gently until soft – about fifteen minutes.

Add the stock, tarragon, herbs, and bay leaves and simmer for another ten minutes.

Meanwhile, clean the mussels (discarding any that are already open or broken) and steam in the wine for ten minutes. Throw out any that don't open. Strain the cooking liquor through muslin and reserve.

When cool enough to handle, remove the mussels, reserving some in their shells for the garnish, if desired.

Add the mussels and wine to the stock.

Add the reserved bacon and heat gently.

Garnish with parsley and any reserved mussels in their shells.

For a boost of sexual essentials ...

Mussels are rich in

zinc and essential fatty acids

Potatoes supply vitamin C

Resto

rative
Soups

The category of restorative soups is where authentic homemade soup lives up to its traditional image. This is peasant food at its heartiest, cheapest, and most nourishing – absolutely overflowing with the special nutrients that you crave to restore your body to health, vigour, and vitality.

Included in this chapter are recipes designed specifically for the times when you're stressed by illness, accidents, surgery, trauma or difficult life events such as death or divorce. During such times, your natural resources become depleted, because fighting your way through any unpleasant situation takes an enormous toll on your body's immune defences and essential stores of nutrients. The object of these recipes is to compensate for any deficiencies, giving you the boost you need to get back to a normal life.

Stimulating a weakened appetite is the first item on any restorative agenda. Even when the thought of food may not appeal, the right soup can still seem appetizing – and it's easy to digest. Believe it or not, the benefits begin to work even before you put that first spoonful to your lips. Just the smell of a pot of soup bubbling away on the stove stimulates the flow of saliva and gastric juices; by the time it's ready, the most jaded of taste buds will have been rekindled, and you'll be ready to take a step on the road to recovery.

Once your appetite has been restored, it's time to address other areas of recuperation. Any form of illness saps both physical and mental strength, and the nutrients you'll find in the following recipes will help restore both. What could be more nourishing, for instance, than a traditional chicken soup such as the one on page 82? With its powerhouse of enzymes and B vitamins, it will help get your mental processes back to peak performance in no time at all. Even the most "high-tech" of doctors now admit that chicken soup is good for the body as well as the soul.

When you feel up to stronger flavours, why not try the combination of garlic and almonds on page 76? It's a powerful restorative concoction. The antibacterial, antiviral, and antifungal constituents of this fabulous bulb provide protection, while the protein, calorie, and mineral content of almonds helps repair damaged cells and provides much-needed energy. In terms of other energy boosters, few foods are better than beans (see Butter bean, parsley, and garlic soup, page 80), while the immune-boosting functions of mushrooms have been a staple of folklore for centuries (see Mushroom and bean broth, page 81).

I'm always amazed at how many people wrinkle their noses in disgust at the merest mention of Brussels sprouts. While they're certainly not the first food that springs to mind as an appetite stimulant, this is a major error. When anyone is recovering from an illness, sprouts should be high on the list of recovery foods. They're full of vitamin C, and, like all members of the cabbage family, provide substantial amounts of highly protective and immune-boosting phytochemicals. Combining them with garlic, parsley, celery, and Stilton (see page 78) provides a healthy, creamy, and easy-to-eat soup that may well change your view of sprouts for ever.

Of all the commonly used vegetables, the one with the most universal reputation as a restorative is the onion – as much a medicine as it is a food. French onion soup (see page 77) is used as a pick-me-up in the street markets of Paris, while in India, Ayurvedic medicine (the word means "life knowledge") advocates hot onion dahl to get you back on your feet.

You don't have to be ill to enjoy these delicious soups. They're great at any time and are all just as valuable for good, all-round nutrition.

Ajo blanco

This traditional garlic soup of southern Spain provides the extreme healing properties of garlic's sulphur compounds. Combined here with the instant energy derived from natural sugars in the grapes and the extra protein from the almonds, the result is a super-restorative bowl of strengthening nutrients.

170g OR 6oz ground almonds

3 tablespoons extra-virgin olive oil

4 cloves of garlic, peeled and very finely chopped

100g OR 3½oz white breadcrumbs

700ml OR 25fl oz water

250ml OR 9fl oz grape juice

100ml OR 3½fl oz organic bio-yoghurt

400g OR 14oz seedless white grapes, halved (and peeled if you can be bothered)

Mix together the almonds, oil, and garlic thoroughly.

Put into a food processor or blender and add half the breadcrumbs, half the water, and half the grape juice.

Whiz until completely combined.

Pour into a clean bowl.

Put the rest of the water and grape juice into the processor or blender – no need to rinse it out.

Add the yoghurt, and pulse about five times until combined.

Pour the yoghurt mixture into the breadcrumb mixture and stir thoroughly.

Leave in the fridge to cool for about an hour.

Serve garnished with halved grapes.

For a speedy recovery …

Garlic is
antibacterial and antifungal

Live yoghurt provides
pro-biotic bacteria that help restore the immune system

French onion soup

One of the most famous of all restorative soups, this traditional French onion recipe will fill your body with a sense of well-being. It's worth looking for some hard goats' cheese, preferably unpasteurized, as it's easy to digest and contains some of the beneficial natural bacteria used in the cheese-making process.

4 tablespoons extra-virgin olive oil

50g OR 1¾ oz butter

4 large onions, peeled and very finely sliced

1.5 litres OR 55fl oz beef or vegetable stock (*see* Chapter 1)

1 large handful of mixed parsley, sage, and thyme leaves, finely chopped

100g OR 3½ oz hard goats' cheese, grated

4 slices cut off a wholemeal baguette

In a large saucepan, heat the olive oil and butter.

Add the onions and sweat over a low heat until thoroughly softened – about fifteen minutes.

Add the stock and herbs, reserving some of the sage.

Simmer for about ten minutes.

Meanwhile, mix the goats' cheese with the reserved sage.

Put the cheese mixture onto the bread and grill until the cheese is bubbling.

Serve the soup with the slices of bread, cheese, and herbs floating on top.

To protect against infection and speed healing …

Onions contain circulation-boosting
phytochemicals

Thyme is rich in thymol,
an antiseptic essential oil

Cheese supplies extra protein and calcium

Brussels sprouts and Stilton soup

What a cornucopia of revitalizing, re-energizing, and restorative nutrients! In addition to the benefits of the sprouts, onions, and garlic, this soup contains a gentle cleansing action from the parsley, and lots of bone- and body-building calcium from the Stilton. By the way, it tastes absolutely fabulous, too.

4 tablespoons extra-virgin olive oil

1 large red onion, peeled and finely chopped

2 cloves of garlic, peeled and finely chopped

2 stalks of celery, finely chopped

1.3 litres OR 45fl oz vegetable stock (*see* page 13)

500g OR 1 lb 2oz Brussels sprouts, cleaned and peeled

300g OR 10½ oz Stilton, rind removed and cubed

1 handful of chopped parsley

In a large saucepan, heat the olive oil over a low heat.

Add the onions, garlic, and celery and sweat gently for five minutes.

Add the stock and Brussels sprouts and simmer until the vegetables are tender – about fifteen minutes.

Liquidize or blend until smooth.

Add the cheese, return to a simmer and cook until the cheese has melted.

Serve immediately, with the parsley scattered on top.

To revitalize the system …

Brussels sprouts are rich in cancer-fighting **phytochemicals**

Garlic and **onions** supply heart-protective and infection-fighting **sulphur compounds**

Olive oil provides healing **vitamin E**

Butter bean, parsley, and garlic soup

Butter beans are a favourite of middle and southern Europe, as well as the southern United States. This soup is especially good when made with chicken stock, as this adds more healing enzymes. The vegetable option is almost as effective – it will provide more skin-restoring betacarotene.

4 tablespoons extra-virgin olive oil

1 large onion, peeled and finely chopped

2 cloves of garlic, peeled and finely chopped

1.5 litres OR 55fl oz chicken or vegetable stock (*see* Chapter 1)

2 x 400g OR 14oz cans butter beans, thoroughly rinsed

2 large handfuls of parsley, very coarsely chopped

In a large saucepan, heat the oil over a low heat.

Add the onions and garlic and sweat gently until softened.

Add the rest of the ingredients.

Simmer until the beans are slightly tender – about fifteen minutes.

Serve with herb croutons (*see* page128).

For a boost of slow-release energy …

Butter beans are rich in

protein, fibre, slow-release energy, B vitamins, and natural plant hormones

that are a valuable aid to women

Parsley is gently diuretic

Mushroom and bean broth

When your body or mind – or worse still, both – have been through the mill, there's no food quite so physically and emotionally restorative as this interesting broth. The subtle flavour and immune-boosting benefits of mushrooms mix perfectly with the more robust kidney beans to help kick-start the body's regulatory mechanisms.

25g OR 1oz dried porcini mushrooms

2 stalks of celery, roughly chopped

2 large leeks, trimmed, washed, and chopped

1 large sprig of sage

3 bay leaves

400g OR 14oz kidney beans, thoroughly rinsed

200g OR 7oz live bio-yoghurt

Soak the mushrooms in 1.5 litres OR 55fl oz freshly boiled water for fifteen minutes.

Strain them, reserving the liquid, and chop them coarsely.

Pour the liquid into a large saucepan and bring back to a simmer.

Add the celery, leeks, sage, and bay leaves.

Simmer for another fifteen minutes.

Strain again and reserve the liquid.

Add the kidney beans and chopped mushrooms and heat for ten minutes.

Stir in the yoghurt and serve.

To soothe both mind and body …

Kidney beans are a source of
protein, restorative energy,
and **natural plant hormones**

Sage contains **essential oils**
that ease digestion and help regulate moods

Chicken soup with matzo dumplings

There cannot be a more renowned natural "kitchen medicine" than this traditional Jewish chicken soup. Used as the key to recovery by generations of mothers and grandmothers, it is surprisingly easy to make, and its soothing flavour makes it ideal as a first choice for any recovery programme.

100g OR 3½ oz unsalted butter

2 organic eggs, beaten

4 teaspoons of parsley and mint, mixed and chopped

90g OR 3¼ oz matzo meal

4 tablespoons warm water

2 litres OR 40fl oz chicken stock (*see* page 15 – no stock cubes allowed here)

Mix all the ingredients, except the stock, thoroughly.

Leave in the fridge for about two hours.

Bring the stock to a gentle simmer.

Roll the refrigerated mix into eight balls – and don't worry if they're very moist.

Drop them into the stock.

Bring back to a simmer.

Leave to simmer for about fifteen minutes.

To speed recovery …

Chicken provides
healing enzymes,
B vitamins, and minerals

Eggs are rich in **restorative vitamin E**

Leek and lentil soup

Like all members of the *Allium* genus of plants, leeks have a long and effective history in the folklore of healing foods. They've been used as a medicinal food since the time of the ancient Romans, and are valued just as much today. If you're recovering from a cold, flu or bronchitis, then this is the soup to choose.

1.5 litres OR 55fl oz vegetable, ham or beef stock (*see* Chapter 1)

200g OR 7oz Puy lentils

1 tablespoon extra-virgin olive oil

200g OR 7oz organic back bacon, cut into thin shreds

3 large leeks, trimmed, washed, and very finely chopped

2 cloves of garlic, peeled and finely chopped

Matzo dumplings (*see* pages 82 or 130)

In a large saucepan, heat the vegetable stock, then pour in the lentils.

Leave them to cook for about twenty minutes.

Meanwhile, in a separate pan, gently heat the olive oil and sweat the bacon for five minutes.

Add the leeks and garlic. Heat very gently until softened.

Once the lentils are tender, add the vegetables and bacon to the stock.

Add the matzo dumplings and simmer for fifteen minutes.

To heal throat and chest infections …

Leeks contain

antibacterial phytochemicals

Lentils supply easily digested **protein**

and essential trace minerals

zinc and selenium

Hauser broth

Back in the 1960s I was privileged to meet a fascinating man called Gaylord Hauser, one of the early pioneers of natural medicine and healthy eating in America. Today, he would be called a guru, as all the great Hollywood stars flocked to him for nutritional advice. He created this recipe as part of his fasting regime, basing it on the cleansing, alkaline soups that were part of the traditional European natural-health movement.

125g OR 4½oz carrot, grated

125g OR 4½oz celery, with leaves, all finely chopped

50g OR 1¾oz spinach, shredded

1 litre OR 35fl oz water or vegetable stock (*see* page 13)

125ml OR 4fl oz tomato juice

1 teaspoon honey

1 small handful of chopped parsley or snipped chives, or a mixture of both

Simmer the vegetables in the water or stock for thirty minutes.

Add the tomato juice and honey and cook for five more minutes.

Liquidize or blend until smooth.

Serve garnished with the parsley or chives.

To cleanse and heal the system …

Celery and **parsley** are effective **diuretics**

Carrots contain healing

betacarotene

Tomatoes are rich in protective **lycopene**

Slimm

ing

Soups

I must admit from the outset that, in principle, I don't advocate extreme slimming diets of any kind. Yes, of course it's true that obesity is a major health problem in the western world, and probably more so in the UK than anywhere else in Europe.

In Britain, obesity currently costs the National Health Service half a billion pounds annually for the treatment of related diseases such as diabetes, respiratory illness, arthritis, high blood pressure, and heart disease. The problem robs the general economy of an additional two billion pounds in lost productivity, sick pay, welfare, and social care. But this isn't an affliction that can be beaten by quick-fix miracle pills, liposuction or surgical intervention. The endless advertisements for "light", "low-fat", "lean", "low-cal", "starch-reduced", and similar meaningless but imaginatively named products give you some idea of the size of the market that has been created to feed the gullible fat.

Look closely, however, and you'll see that virtually every product claiming to help you lose weight – whether pill, potion, spread, ready-meal, or snack – carries the neat little phrase "when used as part of a calorie-controlled diet". The truth is that you can lose just as much weight without buying any of these products. Controlling calories isn't the ultimate answer.

What does work is living mostly on a sensible, well-balanced, and varied diet in which at least fifty per cent of your energy comes from complex carbohydrates, no more than thirty per cent is generated by fat, and around ten per cent is supplied by protein. With few exceptions (and for rare medical reasons), anyone who needs to lose weight can do so by eating a little less and exercising a little more. It's a simple fact that if you cut out two slices of bread and butter a day and walk for fifteen minutes more, you'll lose one pound or just over half a kilo in a week – even if you do nothing else.

In a normal life, there's no room for lunatic dietary regimes such as the cabbage soup diet or the high-protein diet, diets that depend on the shape of your face or your blood group, diets based on bogus allergy tests that tell you you're fat because you're allergic to wheat or dairy products. The whole meaning of the term "diet" has been debased and changed; used properly, the word describes the normal eating patterns of a nation or the specific eating habits of different groups of people or of individuals. It should *never* mean a regime of deprivation, hunger, inadequate nutrition, and misery.

This selection of recipes that can help you lose weight is included to provide you with soups that are low in fat – particularly the unhealthiest saturated fats – but which are full of highly nutritious herbs and vegetables. There are dandelion leaves, to help stimulate the kidneys and get rid of excess fluid; tomatoes, with their protective lycopene and low calorie content; beans and peas, rich in fibre; protein, essential for growth and repair. Then there are the natural plant hormones that help balance the body's hormone systems: particularly important for women approaching or in the menopause, as they help to stabilize the fluctuations that cause weight gain, hot flushes, and other unpleasant symptoms.

In this chapter you'll find root vegetables such as turnips, another rich source of fibre and minerals as well as the bulk that makes them filling and satisfying but not fattening. Then there is brown rice, with its mass of B vitamins, followed by stimulating spices such as horseradish and ginger, both of which speed up the circulation and metabolism.

I've also included some croutons, a bit of Parmesan cheese, a dollop of rouille, a little butter, and some crème fraîche for a taste of luxury. After all, these recipes, like all the others in this book, have been created for your enjoyment as well as your health.

Mixed nettle soup

No, the title isn't a joke. Nettles have been used as a soup-making ingredient for centuries, and form part of a good soup for slimmers. So stop using those highly toxic and dangerous weedkillers and leave space for a clump of nettles and dandelions in your garden – you'll be doing yourself and the environment a favour. Use gloves to pick the tender, new-grown nettle tips and choose the brightest green leaves from the centre of the dandelions for this recipe. This soup will nourish your blood and at the same time help get rid of any puffiness caused by water retention.

100g OR 3½oz young stinging nettles, dandelion leaves, rocket or sorrel (or a mixture of all)

60g OR 2¼oz organic unsalted butter

4 fat spring onions, chopped

4 tablespoons extra-virgin olive oil

150g OR 5½ oz potatoes

1.2 litres OR 40fl oz vegetable stock (*see* page 13)

300ml OR 10fl oz low-fat, live bio-yoghurt

Whiz the mixed leaves in a food processor or blender.

Soften the butter, mix with the chopped leaves, and put into the fridge.

In a large saucepan, sweat the onions gently in the oil.

Peel and cube the potatoes and add to the pan.

Cook gently for two minutes.

Add the stock and simmer for fifteen minutes, or until the potatoes are cooked.

Stir in the yoghurt and liquidize or blend until smooth.

Return to a very low heat, add the leaf mixture, and stir well.

Serve with herb croutons (*see* page 128).

To help eliminate excess fluid …

Nettles are rich in

iron and **vitamin C**

Dandelions are **diuretic**

Easy tomato and basil soup

Who today has the time or patience to peel and deseed fresh tomatoes? This is my favourite quick-and-easy recipe for homemade tomato soup – without the salt, sugar, and additives found in most commercial varieties. This sustaining and filling soup also boasts natural mood-enhancers – just what you need if you're trying your hardest to lose some weight and feeling a bit down in the mouth.

3 tablespoons rapeseed oil

1 medium onion, peeled and very finely chopped

1 clove of garlic, peeled and very finely chopped

1 stick of celery, finely sliced

2 x 400g OR 14oz cans organic, whole plum tomatoes

700ml OR 25fl oz vegetable stock (*see* page 13)

2 tablespoons tomato purée

12 basil leaves

In a large saucepan, heat the oil over a low heat. Add the onion, garlic, and celery and heat gently for about five minutes.

Pour in all of the liquid from the cans of tomatoes.

Add the stock and tomato purée and simmer for about twenty minutes.

Slice the tomatoes lengthwise into quarters. Add to the pan with all the juices.

Simmer for another ten minutes.

Serve with the basil leaves floating on top, or with herb floaters made only with basil leaves (*see* page 131).

For a non-fattening, healthy mood boost …

Celery is **diuretic**

Tomatoes supply cancer-fighting **lycopene**

Basil is rich in mood-enhancing **essential oils**

Spring Roman vegetable soup

This is "Roman" as in modern, stylish Rome, but similar recipes were used many centuries ago, when the city's inhabitants were already very fond of their soups. A bowl of this makes a sustaining meal, enhanced by the good carbohydrates in pasta and the extra protein and calcium from the cheese.

4 tablespoons extra-virgin olive oil

1 large red onion, peeled and finely chopped

3 cloves of garlic, peeled and very finely chopped

1.2 litres OR 40fl oz vegetable stock (*see* page 13 – no stock cubes allowed here)

400g OR 14oz fresh spring green vegetables – any combination of French beans, runner beans, peas or baby broad beans

100g OR 3½oz conchigliette or any other very small pasta

100g OR 3½oz Parmesan cheese, grated

In a large saucepan, heat the oil and gently sweat the onion for five minutes.

Add the garlic and heat for another three minutes.

Pour in the stock and bring to a simmer.

Cut the longer legume vegetables into 1cm OR 0.5-inch pieces.

Add the vegetables to the stock and continue simmering.

Depending on which pasta you're using, add it so that the cooking time for vegetables and pasta coincides.

Serve topped with the grated Parmesan.

To provide a good dose of energy …

Beans and **peas** are a good source of
protein, fibre, slow-release energy,
and **natural plant hormones**

Jerusalem artichoke soup

I once tried making Jerusalem artichoke soup and, delicious though it was, I vowed I'd never do it again – those deformed, gnarled little tubers were a nightmare to peel. Now things are different, as there are new varieties which are almost as smooth-skinned as potatoes, but with the distinctive flavour of artichoke. With the added nutritional bonus of crème fraîche, and partnered by a chunk of bread and a small salad, this soup makes a perfect and energizing meal .

2 stalks of celery, with leaves

1 large onion, peeled and coarsely chopped

700g OR 1lb 9oz Jerusalem artichokes, peeled and cubed

2 large carrots, trimmed and peeled if not organic, cubed

3 bay leaves

1.5 litres OR 55fl oz vegetable stock (see page 13)

1 small handful of chopped chives

200ml OR 7fl oz crème fraîche

Cut the leaves off the celery and reserve. Finely slice the celery stalks.

Put all the ingredients, apart from the celery leaves and crème fraîche, into a large saucepan and simmer until the vegetables are soft – about thirty minutes.

Remove the bay leaves and blend or process until smooth.

Return to the pan and stir in the crème fraîche.

Pour into bowls, add a blob of rouille (see page 129), and serve with the celery leaves floating on top.

NOTE: if you grow your own chives and are making this soup in the summer, chive flowers make an attractive additional accompaniment perched on top of the rouille.

To improve the digestion …

Jerusalem artichokes are rich in
soluble fibre that is extremely satisfying and
filling and also improves digestion

Bay leaves contain essential oils
to help relieve joint pain and improve digestion

Dill and turnip soup

This unusual, peppery soup is both filling and healthy. Turnips are a storehouse of many vital nutrients which, along with their satisfying texture, makes them a good addition to any weight-loss regime. The added health and flavour benefits of parsley and dill are a bonus in this recipe.

4 tablespoons rapeseed oil

1 large onion, peeled and finely chopped

3 cloves of garlic, peeled and finely chopped

500g OR 1 lb 2oz young spring turnips, peeled and cubed

1 litre OR 35fl oz vegetable stock (*see* page 13)

1 teaspoon dried dill

1 handful of chopped parsley

8 sprigs of fresh dill

In a large saucepan, sweat the onion and garlic gently in the oil.

Add the turnip cubes and stir until well-coated.

Pour in the stock and dried dill and simmer for about twenty minutes.

Liquidize or blend until smooth.

Bring back to a simmer, add the chopped parsley, and simmer for five more minutes.

Serve garnished with the sprigs of fresh dill.

For a low-fat dose of nutrients …

Turnips are high in

fibre, calcium, phosphorus, potassium, and B vitamins

Parsley is gently diuretic

Dill helps the digestive process

Celery and brown rice soup

This makes a great winter soup for anyone fighting the battle of the bulge. Add some good wholemeal bread, a mixed green salad, and some fresh fruit and you have a nourishing and filling supper. In addition to the benefits of brown rice and horseradish, the betacarotene and minerals in the red pepper and stock make it a worthy slimming soup.

4 tablespoons extra-virgin olive oil

5 thick stalks of celery, finely chopped

2 cloves of garlic, finely chopped

1 red pepper, deseeded and finely chopped

1.2 litres OR 40fl oz vegetable stock (see page 13)

200g OR 7oz brown rice

1 level teaspoon horseradish sauce

1 handful of parsley

Heat the oil in a large saucepan. Add the celery, garlic, and red pepper and heat gently for five minutes.

Add the stock and bring to a boil.

Reduce to a simmer and add the rice.

Simmer, covered, until the rice is tender – this could take about thirty minutes (brown rice is much more robust than white).

Check the pot every ten minutes or so. If it seems to be getting too dry, add more stock or water.

About five minutes before the soup is ready, add the horseradish and parsley and stir thoroughly.

For a vitamin and energy boost …

Brown rice is rich in
fibre, B vitamins, and **slow-release energy**

Horseradish is a general
digestive and **circulatory stimulant**

Melon and ginger soup

Don't make the mistake of serving this too cold or you'll miss out on the delicate flavour. All melons are gently laxative, while mint is one of the best of all digestive herbs. The ginger provides a boost to the metabolism. This is a perfect and refreshing combination if you're trying to lose a few pounds.

1 cantaloup melon

1 galia melon

400ml OR 14fl oz apple juice

2 tablespoons lemon juice

2 teaspoons ground ginger

1 medium bunch of mint, stalks removed, finely chopped, but reserving four small sprigs

Peel, deseed, and quarter the melons.

Juice one half of each melon by using a juicer, or by cubing and pushing through a fine sieve.

Mix the juiced melon, apple, and lemon juice together with the chopped mint and ginger.

Leave in a cool place, but not in the fridge, for at least an hour.

Use a melon baller or small teaspoon to cut out the flesh of the reserved melon halves.

Add to the mixed juices.

Serve garnished with the mint sprigs.

For a therapeutic boost of vitamin C …

Apples provide **vitamin C, potassium, pectin,** and **malic acid**

Ginger stimulates **circulation**

Good-

mood
Soups

Now, I'm not suggesting that you avoid making the real thing for yourself, but just for a moment, think about all the television advertisements you've seen for soups. The universal theme that links most of these ads is one of happiness, warmth, and comfort.

The images portrayed show the essence of soup and its ability to create good moods: laughing children with mugs of steaming broth on a cold winter's day; happy families sitting down to a tureen of soup thick enough to stand the ladle in; grandparents smiling in gratitude as a nourishing bowl is placed in front of them. Advertising agencies aren't stupid. They know that, buried deep within our psyche, soup is the type of food that brings joy and comfort to those who consume it.

You may find it hard to believe that what you eat can affect your mood, but cast your mind back to your last hangover and how depressed you felt after drinking too much alcohol. On a more positive note, remember how happy you felt after eating a bar of chocolate. Consider the emotional ups and downs you endure when you don't eat properly. By feeding your irritability with a jam doughnut or packet of biscuits, you then find yourself on the roller-coaster ride of wildly fluctuating blood-sugar levels – and all the upsetting mood swings that go with them. What happens to your mood after a wonderful meal with friends or family? How lousy do you feel when you miss breakfast, skip lunch because you're busy, and don't get home until 8.30pm? All of these emotional fluctuations are related to when you eat, what you eat, and how long you go without eating. Even in the busiest of schedules, there is still time for a bowl of soup. In fact, one of the easiest things to take to work is a flask full of this homemade good-mood food. Regardless of any underlying medical problems, eating habits play a large role in overall health. Whether the culprit is poor nutrition, erratic eating patterns or a dependence on high-sugar snacks, sweet canned drinks or gallons of coffee, whether it surfaces at work, school or college, or in the hectic life of a busy mum – so many people find themselves limping through everyday tasks, staggering from highs to lows. By the end of the day, just when they should be at their happiest and joining in with friends, families, and partners, these poor souls are at their moodiest and most miserable.

If these scenarios sound all too familiar, don't despair: this chapter was written especially for you. The soups in this section will help smooth out erratic moods because they provide complex carbohydrates, the best source of slow-release energy that helps keep blood-sugar levels on an even keel. They are also rich in foods containing natural plant chemicals that enhance good moods and lift the spirits, and they're packed full of spices that stimulate both brain and body.

Parsnips, for example – like all the other root vegetables – are a great source of good calories. Green, leafy vegetables, such as spinach and sorrel are rich in iron, which prevents anaemia, one of the most common causes of tiredness, irritability, and depression. Oats and lentils are a major source of the B vitamins that are so important in the prevention of depression and the proper functioning of the brain and central nervous system.

Oily fish such as mackerel contains masses of essential fatty acids. These substances are vital for proper brain development in babies and small children, and are known to function as effective anti-inflammatories in both children and adults. These essential fats are also one of the most important constituents of breast milk, but they only get there if there is enough of them in the mother-to-be's diet.

Spicy parsnip soup

Parsnips, turnips, and swedes are rich sources of slow-release energy, which helps to keep your blood-sugar level on an even keel and prevent mood swings. This soup also gives you a bonus in the form of the instant energy in the honey, making it the perfect soup to take to work for a hot, sustaining lunch.

50g OR 1³/₄oz unsalted butter

1 large onion, peeled and finely sliced

600g OR 1 lb 5oz mixed parsnips, turnips, celeriac, swede, and potatoes, peeled and cubed

3 tablespoons runny honey

1.5 litres OR 55fl oz vegetable stock (*see* page 13)

150ml OR 5fl oz live bio-yoghurt

2 teaspoons garam masala

In a large saucepan, melt the butter over a low heat.

Add the onion and heat gently for five minutes.

Add the vegetables and stir to coat well in the butter.

Remove from the heat and drizzle in the honey, stirring to coat all the vegetables.

Pour in the stock and bring to a boil.

Simmer until the vegetables are tender – about twenty minutes.

Liquidize in a food processor or blender.

Return to the heat.

Stir in the yoghurt and garam masala and heat through.

To provide therapeutic energy …

Parsnips, turnips and swedes are rich sources of **slow-release energy**

Garam masala supplies **mood-elevating** spices

Sorrel soup

Sorrel isn't used nearly as much as it deserves to be. In addition to its mood-enhancing qualities, this delicious herb also works as an effective detoxifier. This recipe is particularly helpful for those suffering from anxiety, especially when it is associated with insomnia – another common cause of mood swings.

2 large handfuls of sorrel, stripped from the stems

55g OR 2oz unsalted butter

4 shallots, peeled and finely sliced

200g OR 7oz potatoes, peeled and cubed

1.2 litres OR 40fl oz vegetable stock (*see* page 13)

400ml OR 14fl oz set Greek yoghurt

Reserve eight leaves of sorrel and whiz the rest briefly in the small bowl of a food processor.

In a small saucepan, melt the butter over a low heat – don't allow it to smoke or burn.

Mix the processed sorrel into the melted butter and leave in the fridge.

Simmer the shallots and potatoes in the stock until tender – about fifteen minutes.

Liquidize or blend the stock mixture until very smooth.

Just before serving, stir in the sorrel and butter mixture and the yoghurt. Heat gently.

Serve topped with potato floaters (*see* page 131).

To soothe and alleviate stressed nerves …

Sorrel is an excellent source of
mood-enhancing **phytochemicals**

Yoghurt supplies brain-soothing **tryptophan**

Pancetta, onion, and green lentil soup

Like all the legumes, lentils are rich in nutrients that fuel and maintain an even metabolism, which in turn promotes a sense of well-being. These components, together with exceptionally high levels of B vitamins and minerals from the other ingredients, make this a rich, filling, and satisfying soup.

4 tablespoons extra-virgin olive oil

1 large onion, peeled and very finely diced

1.2 litres OR 40fl oz ham stock (*see* page 16)

300g OR 10½ oz green lentils, preferably Puy

250g OR 9oz pancetta (or unsmoked bacon) cut in one piece, rind removed, finely cubed

In a large saucepan, sweat the onion gently in three tablespoons of the oil.

Add the stock and bring to the boil.

Pour in the lentils, rinsed if necessary.

Simmer until tender – about fifteen to twenty-five minutes, depending on the variety of lentils.

About five minutes before the soup is ready, fry the pancetta in the remaining oil until crisp.

Drain on kitchen paper.

Serve the soup scattered with the pancetta cubes.

For good general nutrition …

Lentils are an excellent source of
protein and **complex carbohydrates**

Smokie soup

This unusual combination of porridge and smoked mackerel gives a massive mood-boost. In addition to the slow-release energy from the porridge oats and the protein content of the fish, the garlic, leeks, and onion add flavour and loads of protective phytochemicals.

4 tablespoons extra-virgin olive oil

2 large onions, peeled and finely chopped

2 leeks, washed and finely chopped

1 clove of garlic, peeled and finely chopped

1 large carrot, trimmed and peeled if not organic, grated

1 large potato, peeled and grated

500ml OR 18fl oz each fish stock (*see* page 14) and water

4 smoked mackerel fillets (not canned), skinned and boned

55g OR 2oz unsalted butter

100g OR 3½ oz fine porridge oats

4 tablespoons double cream

In a large saucepan, sweat the vegetables gently in the oil until soft – about ten to fifteen minutes.

Add the stock and water mixture and simmer for fifteen minutes.

Poach the mackerel fillets with the butter and just enough water to cover them for about six minutes.

Pour the poaching liquid into the stock.

Flake the fish, add to the soup, and stir in the oats.

Remove from the heat, cover, and leave to stand for ten minutes.

Serve with one spoonful of cream in each bowl.

To boost energy and mood

Mackerel provides
essential fatty acids

Porridge oats are rich in
B vitamins and soluble fibre

Olive oil provides **vitamin E**

Spicy spinach soup

Here is a valuable, nutritious soup that also promotes a good mood. Spinach mixed with lots of chilli (a mood stimulant) and coriander – the essential oils which have enhanced moods for centuries – turns this soup into a nutritional powerhouse, providing vitamins that help keep both mind and body healthy.

4 tablespoons extra-virgin olive oil

2 red onions, peeled and finely chopped

3 cloves of garlic, peeled and finely sliced

1 teaspoon of chopped fresh chilli, all seeds removed

Half a handful each of freshly chopped parsley, mint, and coriander leaves

600g OR 1lb 5oz washed spinach (no need to remove stalks)

1.5 litres OR 55fl oz vegetable stock (see page 13)

200ml OR 7fl oz crème fraîche

In a large saucepan, sweat the onions in the oil for two minutes.

Add the garlic and continue heating for two more minutes.

Stir in the chilli, parsley, mint, and coriander and heat for a further two minutes.

Finely chop the spinach, add to the pan with about three tablespoons of the stock, and heat for another two minutes, stirring continuously.

Add the rest of the stock and simmer for about ten minutes.

Stir in the crème fraîche and serve with Emmental croutons (see page 128).

To lift the spirits …

Spinach is a rich source of

folic acid,

one of the essential **B vitamins**

Winte
wa

r-
rming
Soups

More than any other time of year, winter is the season when we turn naturally to warming soups. During the cold-weather months, your body craves those thick-enough-to-stand-the-spoon-in, rib-sticking, satisfying, and nourishing bowls of homemade goodness.

But the soups in this chapter aren't just designed to warm your hands and fill you with energy-giving, heat-generating calories. These are recipes that actually help protect you against winter's ills. An efficient and effective immune system is vital during cold, damp months, when viruses thrive and opportunistic bacteria wait for any chance they can get to make their home in your nose, throat, sinuses, chest or stomach. A great misconception is that food poisoning is mainly a summer ailment; in fact, this is far from the truth. With central heating running at full tilt and all the windows closed, kitchens are often warmer in winter than they are in summer. People get careless and worry less about getting food into the fridge quickly. Shopping sits around longer before it's unpacked. And when that happens, bacteria have a chance to thrive and multiply.

Seasonal affective disorder (SAD), commonly known as the "winter blues", is another major hazard for many people, and as the days get shorter, their depression gets worse. But it may surprise you that, in addition to the use of antidepressants such as St John's Wort and exposure to high-intensity light, food is another major factor in the relief of the awful depression that is the main symptom of this condition.

That is why some of the winter-warming soups in this chapter contain specific nutrients which help overcome the symptoms of SAD. They do this by elevating moods and providing abundant slow-release energy that helps to keep your blood-sugar level on a more even keel. This, in turn, prevents the sudden drop in blood sugar known as hypoglycaemia, which is frequently a precursor of a downturn in your mood and the start of a depressive episode.

The base for many of these recipes is a variety of root vegetables: good providers of calories from the complex carbohydrates they contain. They are also a rich source of minerals. Some provide abundant amounts of betacarotene, which the body uses as an antioxidant and protective nutrient and also converts into vitamin A, which is essential for natural immunity and healthy skin. A vital function of betacarotene is its role in the maintenance of good night vision – so important for anyone driving during winter.

Traditional ingredients of winter soups include all the legumes. Chickpeas, butter beans, broad beans, and split peas are just some of those used in these recipes, and they have unique nutritional properties. They're an excellent source of protein, and of minerals such as calcium, zinc, and even a little iron. And they also contain varying amounts of phytoestrogens: natural plant hormones that are particularly important for women.

Not surprisingly, herbs and spices feature in these recipes, too. Curry, bay leaves, chilli, and parsley add flavour and warmth. Most important are members of the *Allium* genus of plants: garlic, leeks, and onions. They're antibacterial, antifungal, and antiviral, which means they're hugely protective against virtually all infectious organisms. Their hidden bonus is that they encourage the elimination of cholesterol – especially important during wintertime, when consumption of fatty foods tends to rise. They also help make the blood less sticky, and they help to lower blood pressure.

While all this may sound like a prescription for winter medicine rather than recipes for soups, I assure you that these are the best-tasting prescriptions you'll ever have.

Thick barley and vegetable soup

Barley is a staple food in the Middle East, and in ancient Rome was used in soups to feed the gladiators. Sadly, these days it's mostly ignored in western cooking. This recipe uses whole pot barley, available in most supermarkets and health-food stores, which is a real winter tonic. In contrast, the polished, refined pearl barley provides only calories.

2 tablespoons extra-virgin olive oil

1 large onion, peeled and finely chopped

1 large carrot, trimmed and peeled if not organic, finely cubed

1 large leek, trimmed, washed, and very finely diced

1 litre OR 35fl oz vegetable stock (*see* page 13)

3 bay leaves

5 tablespoons pot barley

1 large handful of chopped fresh parsley

In a large saucepan, heat the olive oil. Add the onion, leeks, and carrots and heat gently for five minutes.

Add the vegetable stock and bay leaves.

Bring to the boil and add the barley.

Simmer for about one hour.

Remove the bay leaves.

Serve with the parsley sprinkled on top.

To supply vital nutrients …

Pot barley is rich in

fibre, calcium, potassium, and B vitamins

Luscious mulligatawny

Like many dishes inherited from the days of the Raj, this soup is not only hot, spicy, and warming, but nutritionally valuable as well.

4 tablespoons extra-virgin olive oil

500g OR 1 lb 2oz mixed carrots, leeks, celery, and parsnips, very finely diced

4 plump spring onions

2 large cloves of garlic, peeled and finely chopped

4 teaspoons green curry paste

1.2 litres OR 40fl oz beef stock (*see* page 17)

1 mango, juiced, or 100ml OR 3½fl oz mango juice

Coat the vegetables in the oil and sweat them in a large, covered saucepan for ten minutes.

Add the curry paste and continue cooking for another ten minutes, stirring occasionally.

Pour in the stock and simmer until the vegetables are tender.

Add the mango juice and heat through.

Serve with herb croutons made with coriander (*see* page 128).

To warm and fortify the consitution …

Beef stock is rich in B vitamins

Leeks, garlic, and onions supply protective phytochemicals

Carrots and mango juice provide vital betacarotene

Vegetable and bean soup

In the middle of winter, you not only need the warming properties of this typical peasant soup, but you'll also benefit from the antibacterial effects of the garlic and onion. A bowlful of this delicious combination will keep you going when you have to shovel the snow away from your door.

4 tablespoons extra-virgin olive oil

1 large onion, peeled and very finely chopped

2 cloves of garlic, peeled and very finely chopped

2 large courgettes, trimmed and grated

4 new potatoes, scrubbed and grated just before use (otherwise they'll discolour)

1 large carrot, peeled and trimmed if not organic, grated

1.5 litres OR 55fl oz vegetable stock (*see* page 13)

2 x 240g OR 8½ oz cans (drained weight) flageolet beans

In a large saucepan, heat the oil. Add the onion and garlic and sweat gently for about five minutes.

Add the grated vegetables and continue heating for five more minutes, stirring continuously and adding a little more oil if necessary.

Pour in the stock and simmer for ten minutes.

Whiz in a food processor or blender until smooth.

Return to the pan.

Rinse the beans thoroughly.

Add to the pan, bring back to a simmer, and heat gently for five more minutes.

Serve with rice fritters (*see* page 130).

For a nutritional energy boost …

Beans and **potatoes** supply masses of
slow-release energy

Carrots are rich in immune-boosting
vitamin A

Chickpea and spicy beef sausage soup

This is the perfect soup to choose if you're suffering from SAD (the winter blues), because it helps improve everything from circulation to mood. The combination of chickpeas and spicy sausage protects your bones during the dark days of winter, improves blood flow, and promotes balanced blood-sugar levels – lifting the spirits as well as treating the taste buds.

3 tablespoons extra-virgin olive oil

1 large onion, peeled and finely chopped

Half a bulb of fennel, finely chopped

1 large bulb of garlic, peeled and finely chopped

300g OR 10½ oz spicy beef sausage, cut into chunks

1.2 litres OR 40fl oz beef stock (*see* page 17)

2 x 240g OR 8½ oz cans (drained weight) chickpeas

In a large saucepan, heat the oil. Add the onion, fennel, and garlic and sweat them until softened.

Add the sausage.

Pour in the stock and chickpeas and simmer until tender – about fifteen minutes.

Remove four tablespoons of the chickpeas and liquidize the rest of the mixture in a food processor or blender.

Return to the heat until boiling.

Serve with the whole chickpeas floating on top.

For all-round nutrition …

Chickpeas are rich in **calcium**

The **beef** in the **sausages** and **stock** provides **protein, iron,** and **B vitamins** which nourish the nervous system

Spanish bean and chorizo soup

Good neighbours can make an enormous difference to your quality of life. My wife, Sally, and I are blessed with the best. Denzil lived for some years in Spain and passed this recipe on to his wife, Vee, who often arrives on our doorstep with a steaming pan of this fabulous taste of Spanish sun to chase away the winter blues.

2 tablespoons extra-virgin olive oil

1 medium onion, peeled and finely chopped and diced

2 cloves of garlic, peeled and finely chopped

1 tablespoon plain flour

1.2 litres OR 40fl oz ham stock (*see* page 16)

1 x 450g OR 16oz can butter beans, rinsed

100g OR 3½ oz broad beans

250g OR 9oz thin chorizo sausage, finely cubed

Heat the olive oil in a large saucepan. Sweat the onion and garlic gently in the oil until softened – about ten minutes.

Stir in the flour and continue stirring for about five minutes.

Pour in the stock very slowly, stirring until the flour takes up the liquid completely.

Add the butter beans and broad beans.

Simmer until the beans are almost tender – about ten minutes.

Add the chorizo and heat through.

To fight off winter depression …

Butter beans and broad beans contain
fibre, protein, minerals, and
natural plant hormones which help elevate mood

Dutch pea soup with smoked sausage

Redolent of those wonderful Dutch paintings of frozen winter scenes, this is another of the great peasant recipes of Europe. Split peas give this soup its unique character, and its consistency of thick porridge. A bowlful with a chunk of bread and a crisp winter salad is all you need for a nourishing lunch or supper. My dear Dutch friend Henri van der Zee has a pea soup party on his birthday every year – but don't wait a year before you try this recipe for yourself.

300g OR 10½oz split green peas

40g OR 1½oz unsalted butter

200g OR 7oz smoked back bacon, finely chopped

1 medium onion, peeled and coarsely chopped

1.5 litres OR 55fl oz ham stock (*see* page 16)

500g OR 1 lb 2oz good smoked sausage, rind removed and cut into chunks

Soak the peas in plenty of water overnight.

In a large saucepan, melt the butter and sauté the bacon gently for two minutes.

Add the onion and continue heating for four more minutes.

Stir in the soaked peas, add the stock, and simmer, covered, until the peas are soft – between one and two hours.

Mix in the sausage and simmer for another ten to fifteen minutes.

NOTE: this robust soup can also be served cold, with any fat skimmed from the top.

For warmth and energy …

Split peas are rich in
fibre and minerals

Sausage supplies vital protein

Soup

Garn

ishes

The function of the garnishes in the following pages is to provide added value to the recipes listed in the rest of this book. They help to turn super soups into extra-super soups, by adding substance and a bonus of nutrients.

They are all simple to make, too. Once you've grasped the basics, you'll have no trouble in devising your own recipes that include the family's favourite ingredients. Adding the more substantial garnishes, such as dumplings, will turn a simple bowl of soup into a satisfying meal – which is, of course, the historical basis for their inclusion. Dumplings of all sorts are a feature of peasant cooking around the world. From the Russian steppes to the green pastures of rural Ireland, from the Victorian England of Mrs Beeton to family kitchens in China and Japan, dumplings were the traditional way poor people stretched their limited food supply to fill the stomachs of their hungry families.

In the UK, the usual method for making dumplings is to mix self-raising flour with half the amount of shredded suet, then add salt, pepper, assorted herbs, and just enough water to make a dough firm enough to roll into balls. The *grand'mères* of Brittany make their dumplings with buckwheat, which is ideal for those on a gluten-free diet. To make one large dumpling, they combine 500g (1lb 2 oz) of buckwheat flour, a pinch of salt, four eggs, a nob of softened butter, two tablespoons of caster sugar, lots of black pepper, 150ml (5fl oz) of milk, and two tablespoons each of raisins and chopped prunes with enough water to make a thick batter. Then they wrap it in a tea towel and cook it in the soup.

Japanese cooks are a little more subtle, and their staple rice-flour dumplings are gluten- and wheat-free. Called *dango*, they are made with *shiratamako* (glutinous rice flour).

One favourite recipe combines rice flour with cooked, mashed pumpkin and lotus root, which is then rolled into small balls, deep-fried, and tipped into the simmering soup.

In Italy, the favourite garnish is (naturally) pasta. As well as plain pasta, ravioli is often added to soups, and sometimes meatballs make a filling choice. History tells us that Marco Polo brought the idea of pasta back to Italy, so it's hardly surprising that the Chinese make fabulous dumplings from a mixture of mushrooms, bean sprouts, pak choi, ginger, spring onions, and eggs wrapped in a flour-and-water dough – just like ravioli.

The following dumplings and croutons will make your soups more filling and also add nutritional value. You'll get plenty of calcium, fibre, and B vitamins from Emmental croutons, for example, digestive benefits from essential oils in the Herb croutons, and a little extra iron and protein from Matzo dumplings. Even the Rouille provides fantastic nutritional qualities. This spicy garlic sauce used for fish soup and bouillabaisse is often avoided because some people think it's unhealthy, yet it contains masses of vitamin C and betacarotene from the pepper, lycopene from the tomatoes, heart protection from the garlic, cancer-fighting properties from the turmeric, and some vitamin E for skin and circulation from the olive oil.

The floater recipes might sound odd, but my wife and I devised these as a simple, delicious way of adding body and nutrients to any soup. Onion floaters will help with any form of cold, cough or chest infection. Use the Beetroot floaters for anyone with anaemia, or after surgery, when there may have been blood loss; they're great for women, too, especially just before, during, and after periods. The thyme in the Potato floaters adds antiseptic value to the extra energy that they supply, while the Courgette floaters contain betacarotene.

Use the following recipes, be inventive with your own, and you'll get even more super nutrients from my super soups.

Emmental croutons

Add to clear soups for extra calcium and protein, as well as the nutrients in the wholemeal bread.

2 tablespoons extra-virgin olive oil

4 slices of stale organic wholemeal bread

125g OR 4½oz Emmental cheese

In a frying pan, heat the oil until slightly smoking.

Remove the crusts from the bread and cut into 1cm OR 0.5-inch cubes.

Grate the cheese finely.

Roll the bread in the cheese, pressing it in firmly.

Fry in the oil, turning continuously, until golden on all sides.

Herb croutons

Use different herbs for their specific properties.

85g OR 3oz wholemeal breadcrumbs

2 teaspoons fresh, soft herbs (mint, parsley, sorrel, coriander, basil, but not tough herbs such as rosemary), finely chopped

1 small organic egg, whisked

3 tablespoons extra-virgin olive oil

Mix the breadcrumbs with the herbs.

Form into small balls about the size of an acorn, then flatten with your hands.

Dip into the egg and drain.

In a frying pan, heat the oil until smoking slightly.

Fry the bread balls until slightly golden – about two minutes.

Rouille

Not just the delicious traditional French essential for fish soup, but a garnish bursting with heart-protective, cancer-fighting lycopene, garlic, and turmeric.

Half a red pepper, peeled and deseeded

100g OR 3½ oz canned tomatoes, drained of most, but not all, liquid

3 cloves of garlic, peeled

2 thick slices of organic wholemeal bread, soaked in water

1 teaspoon turmeric

75ml OR 2½ fl oz extra-virgin olive oil

Whiz the pepper, tomatoes, and garlic in a food processor or blender.

Add the bread and process again.

Whisk the turmeric into the olive oil.

Pour the olive oil mixture gradually into the food processor or blender, pulsing until smooth.

Matzo dumplings

These contain good carbohydrates, energy, and extra nutrients. Use them to turn your soup into a more sustaining meal.

100g OR 3½ oz unsalted butter

2 organic eggs, beaten

4 teaspoons parsley and mint, chopped and mixed

90g OR 3¼ oz matzo meal

4 tablespoons warm water

Mix all the ingredients thoroughly.

Leave in the fridge for about two hours.

Roll the mix into eight balls – and don't worry if they're very moist.

Drop them into the soup.

Bring back to a simmer.

Leave them to cook for about fifteen minutes.

Rice fritters

Give additional protein, calcium, iron, and B vitamins to any soup with these fritters.

1 large organic egg

100g OR 3½oz cooked rice
(left over from a previous meal
is perfect)

4 tablespoons grated
Parmesan cheese

1 tablespoon soft herbs: parsley,
sage, tarragon

200g OR 7oz unsalted butter

Beat the egg.

Mix the rice with the cheese and stir in enough egg
to make it stick together.

Add the herbs and mix thoroughly again.

Put the mixture into your palms and roll until gooey.

Separate into small balls. Flatten until they're about the size
of a fifty-pence piece.

Leave in the fridge for an hour.

Melt the butter in a frying pan.

Fry the fritters for about five minutes on each side.

Floaters

This is the basic recipe for the most wonderful addition to many of the soups in this
book. Add the herbs as suggested or make up ideas of your own, but any herbs you add
must be soft herbs such as parsley, sage, mint, tarragon – not woody herbs like rosemary.

150g OR 5½oz wholemeal flour

1 organic egg , whisked

Freshly ground black pepper:
2 turns from a pepper mill

6 tablespoons extra-virgin
olive oil

Beat the flour into the egg. Add the pepper.

Grate the vegetables to be used (*see* page 131). Squeeze out
as much water as possible, squash them into walnut-sized balls,
then flatten until they're about 1cm OR 0.5-inches thick.

Coat them in the batter mixture.

Heat the oil and gently sauté them for three minutes on each side.

Potato floaters

Use about 100g (3½oz) of baking potato; be sure to rinse after grating to get rid of the starch. Add three teaspoons fresh, chopped thyme. Potatoes are a good source of extra vitamin C. Thymol, the essential oil in thyme, is a powerful antibacterial.

Courgette floaters

Use about 200g (7oz) of courgettes, trimmed but not peeled. Add three tablespoons of chopped flat-leaf parsley. Extra betacarotene from the courgette skin, combined with the gentle diuretic effect of parsley, makes these good for skin problems.

Beetroot floaters

Use 100g OR 3½oz of freshly grated raw beetroot mixed with one teaspoon of horseradish. One of the best blood boosters, beetroot is used in eastern Europe to treat anaemia.

Onion floaters

Use one *very* finely grated onion, or three large grated spring onions, with two teaspoons of chopped fresh oregano. Choose these for extra protection against infections, coughs, and colds, and for the mood-boosting and antiseptic properties of oregano.

Soup

Hea

ling

If I've learned one thing after nearly forty years of working with patients, twenty-five years presenting *BodyTalk*, a radio phone-in show, on London's LBC, and twenty years answering readers' questions in the *Daily Express*, *Woman* magazine, and many other journals, it's that the general population has an enormous thirst for knowledge.

Amazingly, I'm still being asked questions which, in all these years, have never been asked before. But whatever the questions, they nearly all have one thing in common. When ordinary men, women, mothers, fathers, grandparents (and growing numbers of children and teenagers) phone in or write, they're looking for help for an illness or an explanation of a symptom. That's the reason these healing charts are included in *Super Soups*. I'm certain that many of you looking at this book for the first time will have turned straight to this section to see if there is a remedy for your specific problem. If the pharmacy is your first port of call for the relief of minor ailments, it may come as a surprise that there could be healing benefits in a bowl of soup. Older readers, however, may well remember their grandmothers' reliance on these and other traditional "kitchen remedies".

As a naturopath, I've embraced kitchen medicine as part of my philosophy since my college days. It is a branch of medicine based on principles that stretch back to man's earliest beginnings. In fact, the whole ethos of "food as medicine" grew out of the use of herbs and plants by medicine men and witchdoctors. It is found in religious teachings such as those of the priests of antiquity in Egypt, the earliest monks and nuns of Christianity, the ancient traditions of Ayurveda in India, and the healing mystics of the

Jewish Cabbala. It also appears in the wonders of Tibetan medicine and the medicinal foods of traditional Chinese medicine. This common principle was encapsulated in the words of Hippocrates, the father of modern medicine, when he wrote: "Man should let his food be his medicine, and his medicine be his food." So, if this your first venture into using foods to heal, you are joining a long, ancient, and worthy tradition.

Food provides your body with the essential protein, carbohydrates, vitamins, and minerals it needs to survive. But food consists of much more than these basic nutrients. Plants, for example, contain hundreds of natural chemical substances, many of which have specific therapeutic benefits. In earlier times, people discovered these benefits by chance, and the value of particular plants was taught and handed down from generation to generation. No one knew why onion or garlic soothed a cough, for example, or liver and carrots could make you see in the dark, but they made use of that knowledge. No one understood the reasons why mint relieved indigestion, shellfish made men sexy, or lettuce helped induce sleep; they simply used this knowledge and passed it on.

Happily, in the twenty-first century there has been a massive increase in interest in the medicinal properties of food. Hardly a week goes by without the publication of new research in the world's leading medical journals, where we can read that tomatoes help control prostate cancer, wholegrain cereals prevent heart disease, garlic lowers cholesterol, oily fish improves brain development in babies and reduces the pain of arthritis… the list is almost endless.

So whatever your health problem, there will surely be a herb, spice or foodstuff that can help. Some will reduce the severity of symptoms, others will protect against degenerative diseases, and still others could prevent a recurrence of distressing or even life-threatening conditions.

Soup Healing Charts

Condition	Healing foods	Effect
Acne	Cabbage	Is rich in antibiotic sulphur compounds
	Fennel	Improves fat digestion
	Garlic, onions	Are antibacterial
Anaemia	Nettles, watercress	Are rich in iron and the vitamin C required for iron absorption
	Red meat	All red meats contain easily absorbed iron
Anxiety	Basil, rosemary	Contain calming essential oils
	Bread, dairy products	Encourage the brain's production of feel-good hormones
Arthritis	Oily fish	Essential fatty acids in oily fish are natural anti-inflammatories
	Celery	Eliminates uric acid
	Broccoli, turnips	Supply protective antioxidants
Asthma	Garlic, onions, leeks	Are natural decongestants
	Watercress	Is rich in unique lung-protective chemicals
	Olive oil	Provides vitamin E – essential for healthy lung tissue
Back pain	Thyme	Is a muscle-relaxant
	Oily fish, mussels	Provide natural anti-inflammatories
	Chillies, curry	Stimulate blood flow and speed healing
Bronchitis	Garlic, onions, leeks	Are powerful antibacterials and decongestants
	Coriander, thyme	Are expectorant and decongestant
Catarrh	Garlic, onions, leeks	Are powerful antibacterials and decongestants
	Coriander, thyme	Are expectorant and decongestant
Chilblains	Sorrel, basil, garlic, coriander, chilli	All these herbs and spices help improve the circulation
Cholesterol	Garlic, onions, leeks, chives	All, especially garlic, help lower cholesterol
	Oats, beans	Provide special fibre which also reduces cholesterol levels

Condition	Healing foods	Effect
Chronic fatigue	Basil, bay, sage	All are mood-enhancing
	Beans, lentils, barley, oats, rice, bread	Beans and cereals provide good energy
	Eggs, meat, fish, poultry	All are needed for protein
Circulation problems	Sorrel, basil, garlic, coriander, chilli	All these herbs and spices help improve the circulation
Colds	Garlic, onions, leeks	Are decongestant and protect against secondary infections
	Chives, thyme, sage, rosemary	Essential oils in these herbs are antiviral
	Shellfish	Contain immune-boosting zinc
Constipation	Nettles, sorrel	Are gentle laxatives
	Beans, lentils, oats, barley	Are rich sources of fibre, which improves colonic function
Cough	Garlic, onions, leeks	Are powerful antibacterials and decongestants
	Coriander, thyme	Are expectorant and decongestant
Cystitis	Garlic	Is antibacterial and antifungal
	Celery, parsley	Both are gentle, cleansing diuretics
Depression	Basil, rosemary	Are mood-enhancers
	Oats, red meat, beans, lentils	All are excellent sources of B vitamins, essential for the nervous system
Diarrhoea	Mint	Soothes the digestive tract
	Garlic	Helps fight the food-poisoning bacteria
	Rice, carrots	Are easily digested and non-irritant
Diverticulitis	Garlic	Helps prevent infection
	Mint	Soothes the digestive tract
	Rice, carrots	Are easily digested and non-irritant
Flatulence	Fennel, mint, coriander	All contain essential volatile oils which improve digestion and reduce flatulence

Condition	Healing foods	Effect
Fluid retention	Parsley	Is one of the most effective natural diuretics. Use generously
	Celery	Is a gentle diuretic
Gallstones	Sage, fennel, tarragon	All aid fat digestion and reduce stone-causing cholesterol
	Parsnips, turnips, brown rice, oats	Are excellent sources of soluble fibre, which speeds the removal of cholesterol
Gingivitis	Cherries, tomatoes	Are rich in immune-boosting vitamin C
	Thyme	Is a powerful antiseptic
	Prawns	Provide zinc, essential for good resistance
Gout	Celery, parsley, turnips	All reduce levels of uric acid
	Nasturtium flowers	Contain mustard oils, which relieve pain
	Shellfish	Help reduce inflammation
Hair problems	Pak choi	Contains sulphur and vitamin C
	Nettles, rosemary	Both are antiseptic (good in shampoos, too)
	Meat, poultry	Provide iron and B vitamins
	Fish, shellfish	Provide iodine for thyroid function, often a factor in hair problems
Headache	Dandelion leaves	Are diuretic, helping headaches caused by fluid retention
	Rosemary, mint	Are mood-altering herbs that help stress-related headaches
	Garam masala, curry, chilli	Improve blood-flow to the brain for the relief of migraines
	Barley, potatoes	Contain starch, which keeps blood sugar on an even keel
Heartburn	Mint, dill	Contain natural antacid essential oils
	Yoghurt	Provides good bacteria, which aid digestion
	Rice, carrots	Are traditional naturopathic foods for all digestive upsets
Heart disease	Garlic	Helps reduce cholesterol, blood pressure, and the risk of clots
	Ginger, chilli, curry	Stimulate circulation
	Beans, wholegrain cereals	Reduce cholesterol
	Oily fish	Is cardio-protective

Condition	Healing foods	Effect
Hepatitis	Artichokes	Are a source of cynarin, which helps liver function
	Sage, tarragon, horseradish	All improve fat digestion
Herpes	Garlic, leeks	Both are traditional remedies for herpes and are believed to contain antiviral substances
Hypertension	Garlic	Phytochemicals in garlic are beneficial to good blood pressure
	Parsley, celery	Reduce fluid retention
	Wholegrain cereals	Help control cholesterol, often a factor in hypertension
Indigestion	Mint, dill, fennel	All help improve digestion owing to their essential oils
	Carrots, sweet potatoes	Both are rich in healing betacarotenes
	Yoghurt	Improves digestion and prevents flatulence
Influenza	Chicken soup	The traditional flu healer, rich in protein and protective enzymes
	Ginger, turmeric, chilli	Speed the elimination of toxins
	Wholegrain cereals	Provide B vitamins to prevent post-flu depression
Insomnia	Lettuce	Contains mildly soporific chemicals
	Basil	Is wonderfully calming
	Milk, yoghurt, fromage frais, crème fraîche, poultry, oily fish	All supply sleep-inducing tryptophans
Laryngitis	Sage, rosemary	Contain essential oils that are specifically antibacterial to the bugs that commonly cause throat problems
Menstrual problems	Sorrel, nettles	Provide iron to prevent anaemia
	Celery, parsley	Ease uncomfortable fluid retention
	Oily fish	Is anti-inflammatory, for pain relief
	Cherries	Are rich in potassium
	Beans	Are a source of phytoestrogens, which reduce hormonal fluctuations

Condition	Healing foods	Effect
Mouth ulcers	Garlic	Helps with healing
	Yoghurt	The good bacteria in yoghurt help prevent ulcers
	Basil, rosemary, pasta, rice, bread, potatoes	Are all stress-relievers: important as ulcers are mostly stress-induced
Obesity	Most of the super soups	Good soups are filling and sustaining as they provide slow-release energy, which prevents fluctuations in blood sugar and food cravings
Raynaud's syndrome	Basil, sorrel, coriander, garlic, chilli	All help improve the circulation
Restless legs	Watercress, nettles, red meat, green, leafy vegetables	Contain iron to prevent anaemia, a common cause of this condition
SAD	Basil, rosemary	Both contain mood-enhancing essential oils
	Oats	Are rich in antidepressant B vitamins
	Starchy foods	Increase levels of mood-enhancing tryptophan
Sinusitis	Onions, garlic, leeks	Are powerful antibacterials and decongestants
	Coriander, thyme	Both are expectorant and decongestant
Varicose veins	Ginger, chilli, curry, garam masala	All stimulate and improve circulation
	Broccoli	Is a rich source of vein-protecting betacarotene and other antioxidants
	Lentils, beans, barley, oats	All prevent constipation, a common cause of varicose veins

Index

Acknowledgments

As always, I have to thank my wife, Sally, who spent many hours with her head over an endless succession of steaming saucepans developing these delicious recipes. I must also thank Jamie Ambrose for patiently editing yet another of my books – and especially Lara Maiklem and Hilary Lumsden at Mitchell Beazley for not getting angry when my e-mails didn't get through. Special thanks go to Nicki Dowey for her excellent and imaginative photography and the design team for their creative input.